Grey Zone Change

YABOME GILPIN-JACKSON

DEDICATION

To those who point us to new horizons by leading and facilitating Grey Zone Change.

CONTENTS

Table of Tables

Table of Figures

ACKNOWLEDGEMENTS

Every writing project, no matter how small, becomes a reality because of a myriad of conversations and an abundance of support. This guidebook is no exception. I wish to thank the following scholars and practitioners who continue to inspire, encourage, and support me every day. You push me to go deeper and broader and to refine and share my thinking, even when I am not sure what is worth sharing. Among others, I especially thank and acknowledge Dr. Gervase R. Bushe and Dr. Robert Marshak, Susan Marie Good, Tricia Hollyer, Melissa Crump, Teresa Belluz, Fodé Beaudet, Laura Wesley, and Julian Chender for the conversations, peer reviews, and inspiration that have informed this guidebook.

PREFACE

I envision the Grey Zone of Change within the metaphor of journeying through a tunnel. Imagine looking around at everything you know and understand and choosing instead to enter a tunnel that promises new possibilities. You may only be equipped with a flashlight and the company of fellow sojourners. You have no idea what is on the other side, but you have seen enough signals suggesting that the current state is changing and that new opportunities are emerging—if you step into the tunnel and make it through. Sometimes you enter willingly. Other times, circumstances force you into it. Whatever the case may be, you have three choices. You can keep trying to go back to the world you know. You can anxiously try to anticipate whatever comes your way, coping and adapting. Or you can embrace the journey, work with others, try things out, learn what works and what doesn't, and watch the light at the end of the tunnel emerge. This book is for people who embrace the journey. This is the Grey Zone of Change.

Most of us are well-practiced in navigating the grey zone. It is uncannily like life. We are born not knowing how our lives will unfold. We have to content ourselves with signals and clues based on when, where, and to whom we were born. We then embark on the journey of constructing our lives through our relationships, starting with our parents. Our lives advance and emerge as we live them and make choices. Not only is negotiating a series of tunnels how an individual story unfolds, but it is also how humanity has changed and developed over time. It is the human story.

The grey zone experience is equally true of our organizational lives, more so than ever as the world of work becomes more and more complex. The structured models we have known and have been taught to use to solve organizational problems no longer work in all circumstances. There are few black and white scenarios remaining; we are in grey space. It can be disorienting to figure out how to navigate this complex world. We are being challenged to live, to work, and to undergo change differently.

As an emerging Organization Development (OD) practitioner, I had a dissonance experience which led to my thinking and theorizing about the Grey Zone of Change. It is an experience I suppose that most professionals have in a world of work where the level of complexity they encounter is greater than what they had expected. It is the encounter at that intersection where:

Theory Meets Practice
Plans Meet Emergence
Values Meet Dilemmas
Emerging Futures Meet Current Realities

I had been working in a complex healthcare context, with a scenario that included:

- Regionalization of services across four organizations
- Leadership team and role restructures
- Multiple levels of staff transition
- Service delivery changes
- A $10-million cost savings target
- Government-required reporting

Every project meeting I attended was rife with tension. I was asked to support the leader running the initiative. The executive I reported to told me that this was a high-profile project and she would do all she could to help me to be successful. At our first meeting, the responsible operational leader said candidly that he was not a very patient man and that he preferred clear plans and structures to help him move the work forward. However, he also said that he had done enough leadership study to understand that due process was needed to prepare the leaders reporting to him to make it through the required changes. He saw that they were at various stages of preparation and development and would need support to get through the changes collectively. Some structural changes that impacted the leaders had already been made and operational planning to achieve the financial targets was already underway. He said that he was willing to defer to my consulting advice rather than bulldozing through at this point. He needed to do everything from vision-setting, realigning the newly restructured leadership team, and implementing strategies to achieve the savings targets within the year. He realized he needed help to think through it all; he needed a structured yet adaptable approach.

On instinct, I drew out a roadmap for the next year that outlined these stages:

1. Individual Leader Development
2. Team Development Sessions
3. Planning for Change and Transition
4. Joint Visioning
5. Strategic Planning [and implementation] to achieve the Vision
6. Sustaining the Change

He looked at my notepad, appeared satisfied and said: "Yes, as long as we got each step right, that should keep us moving."

My next stop was to meet with a colleague, a fellow OD consultant from one of the other health organizations affected by the regionalization. We were to work together to define a shared approach, to deliver sessions, and to work jointly at both organizations. My colleague was prepared for our meeting. He asked that we embark on a learning conversation (Bushe, 2010) before we proceeded with any planning. He was concerned because he subscribed to a certain approach to OD and wanted to make it clear that it was the only way he wished to work. This approach involved employing large-scale change methodologies and facilitating essential conversations that arise from asking great questions that are often unspoken, thereby impeding success. I assured him that I subscribed to the same approach to facilitating change and transformation, bearing in mind that the client also required rigor and structure alongside these emergent ways of working. There was too much grey area, too much urgency, and too much uncertainty to embark on an exclusively planned or exclusively emergent approach. We needed to stay flexible and open to all the daily changes that were occurring. I showed him my scratched-out pathway and asked—"What if we designed for each of these stages in a way that provided structure, "diagnosis," and a planned approach, as well as space for the important dialogues and the flexibility to be emergent as things changed?"

By the end of the conversation, we had agreed that we did not subscribe to a certain OD methodology but to a certain way of working. I did not realize at the time that we had just agreed to operate from a Dialogic OD mindset in the Grey Zone of Change. We were both energized. We delivered a successful transformation over the next year; the savings target was successfully met and the leadership goals were fulfilled across the board.

This scenario was the genesis of my thinking about the Grey Zone of Change, a term I coined in debriefing our learnings and in writing it up as a case study. Fast forward 10 years. As I review my body of work since then, I am struck by five things:

1. More often than not, I am working in situations involving the Grey Zone of Change.
2. When I have operated from a Dialogic OD mindset, I have grown and found success as a practitioner.
3. Success in the grey zone is characterized by transformational change outcomes.
4. Transformational change outcomes require the development of leaders and all involved, as well as the development or maturation of the collective.
5. I have synthesized the process I scratched out on that notepad into the following three stages: Initiating the Dialogic Inquiry (i.e. individual leader/team development and planning for change and transition), Facilitating the Dialogic Journey (e.g. visioning, strategy, planning and various design sessions), and Sustaining the Transformation.

I have two published case studies about facilitating in the Grey Zone of Change, about the experience of preparing leaders and clients for Dialogic OD through a transformative learning lens, with facilitated grey zone sessions and conversations with OD and change practitioners globally (Gilpin-Jackson, 2013, 2015; Gilpin-Jackson & Crump, 2018). When I submitted the first case study for review in what is now called the *Organization Development Review,* John Vogelsang, the editor, said that, while I did not reference it, I seemed to be talking about Dialogic OD and how it intersects with traditional Diagnostic OD. He referred me to Dr. Gervase Bushe with whom I had already worked with as a graduate student, which led to my introduction to Dialogic OD as the mindset that informs my practice. It was through exploring the question, "Can Diagnostic and Dialogic OD co-exist and be used as complementary forms of engagement in practice?" (Oswick, 2009), that I arrived at my thinking and conceptualizing of the grey zone. This guidebook synthesizes and builds on my previous works to propose ways of understanding, navigating, and facilitating in the Grey Zone of Change, using lessons from my experiences as an executive leader and as a practitioner in leadership and organizational development.

My hope is that you will experience this book as a companion on your journey through the Grey Zone of Change and as a valuable guide to its infinite possibilities. A number of metaphors come to mind—the caterpillar becoming a butterfly, a child emerging from the birth canal, or a seed becoming a tree—to remind us of why this work matters. Butterflies, each with unique patterns on beautifully-coloured wings, miraculously materialize from a larva and a cocoon process that yields between 15,000 and 20,000 species. However, if you force the cocoon open prematurely, the butterfly dies. Seeds of every kind require the right conditions of soil, water, and light to grow. And for humans, a perfect reminder of the emergent nature of life is right there at our beginning, through conception, in-vitro growth and birth. While sharing the DNA of those who came before us, each one of us is unique. Each one of us is alive, having endured incredible odds that could have precluded our very existence[1]. This miracle of life has already taught us all we need to know about the Grey Zone of Change, that space between Point A and Point B. Life and nature have taught us that, for anything to come into being, the conditions must be right for cocooning, growth, and metamorphosis. Then a new, beautiful reality can emerge. The question is:

What new possibility are you willing to pursue through the journey of your Grey Zone of Change?

---

[1] The odds of being alive have been popularly calculated at one in 400 trillion or an even smaller probability. See: Are You a Miracle? On the Probability of Your Being Born: https://www.huffpost.com/entry/probability-being-born_b_877853

INTRODUCTION

Have you ever found yourself in a scenario where:

1. Transformation is required in the way people work, think and behave.
2. There are plenty of questions.
3. There are no clear answers.
4. There are new things to consider regularly.
5. The end goal and solutions are unknown.
6. Processes and progress are emergent.
7. Many people are involved.
8. Everything seems chaotic.

These attributes characterize the Grey Zone of Change. a time in organizations when strategic questions or projects encompass these characteristics, and everyone is trying to figure out the best way forward. A few different terms have been used to describe the types of challenges associated with these scenarios—adaptive challenges, wicked problems, complex and chaotic environments, and VUCA (volatility, uncertainty, complexity and ambiguous) circumstances (Heifetz, Linsky, & Grashow, 2009; Snowden & Boone, 2007). In my experience, the circumstances surrounding these challenges all comprise the same large grey area, where there is no clear pathway. *A space between the current state and the emerging future that is undefined and unknowable.*

Embracing the Grey Zone of Change is our new way of life. It is the new normal in our fourth industrial revolution. The constant and growing need for change and complexity has been well-documented, as has the statistic that 70% of change efforts fail. This guidebook focuses on how to navigate the Grey Zone of Change from a Dialogic Organization Development (OD) mindset, which has proven to be the most successful approach when transformational change is required (Bushe & Nagaishii, 2018).

I have found very few practical resources to guide me through grey zone experiences. Therefore, I have drawn on a variety of theories, resources, and networks in order to make my way. In addition to core OD studies, practice, and ongoing certifications, I have delved into Transformative Learning Theory and Positive Organizational Scholarship, I have become a Human Systems Dynamics Practitioner and a Certified Coach, and I have drawn from the body of work of Liberating Structures (Cameron & McNaughtan, 2016; Human Systems Dynamics Institute, 2019a; Lipmanowicz &

McCandless, 2013; Taylor, Cranton, & Associates, 2012). Each of these areas of theory and practice exists in separate communities that are intersecting and becoming recognizable under the Dialogic OD banner proposed by Bushe and Marshak (2015a).

I have frequently been asked to teach graduate courses to give students experiences in planning and facilitating Dialogic Organization Development methodologies. Usually, they have studied it as a theory for working in complex, collaborative and emergent change, but are not clear about how to apply it in practice. In those instances, I have gone to three key resources—*Dialogic Organization Development,* the groundbreaking book cataloging theory and conceptual application of the field (Bushe & Marshak, 2015a); *The Change Handbook* (Holman, Devane, & Cady, 2007; and its corresponding Collaborative Change Library), which collated a wide range of practical methodologies (https://nexus4change.com/); and online catalogues of models like Liberating Structures (http://www.liberatingstructures.com/) and Human Systems Dynamics (https://www.hsdinstitute.org/resources.html), which cover significant depth and breadth of theory and practice. Grey Zone Change is meant to be a smaller, more condensed guidebook about the process within which these methodologies are used to facilitate transformations. It is not meant to be another inventory of methodologies.

Grey Zone Change is a guidebook because emergent transformation work, by its very nature, cannot be put into a "how to" or prescriptive framework. It is intended to fill in the gap in existing works that provide either the theoretical base or the methodological processes for navigating complex change. It specifically names the Grey Zone of Change as a bridge between the ideals of planned and emergent change. It provides a synthesis of the basic theory and practical approaches to understanding, navigating, and facilitating transformation in the Grey Zone of Change.

Who is this Guidebook For?

This guidebook is for anyone leading transformations in situations characteristic of the Grey Zone of Change. It is written from my perspective as a leader constantly working in the Grey Zone of Change in the public sector and in communities facing social and global marginalization. I also share my perspectives as an OD consultant who supports other leaders in change and transformation. Grey Zone Change is for formal and informal leaders trying to make sense of complexity and chaos in our world, as well as for OD and other practitioners supporting leaders of change and transformation.

What You Will Learn

This guidebook is designed to do the following.
1. Provide an overview of the Grey Zone of Change.
2. Unpack the dynamics of the Grey Zone of Change.
3. Explore how to navigate the Grey Zone of Change in living, leading, and facilitating transformations.
4. Describe a suggested framework and processes for facilitating transformation in the Grey Zone of Change.

Assumptions and Definitions

Grey Zone Change offers an Organization Development (OD) approach to achieving transformational change and development. Readers therefore require a basic understanding of OD, as well as some key technical and everyday terms, which are listed below.

Grey Zone of Change is *defined as the space between an existing system and an emerging or envisioned one that is currently undefined and unknowable.* By system, I mean the way a defined whole is organized (by design or by default) to achieve its specific functions. The Grey Zone of Change applies to situations of complexity, where there are more unknown than known factors about the present and the future. The grey zone applies specifically within complex adaptive systems made up of many parts or "agents" (human, material/technical, technological and/or environmental) that are interacting in connected yet independent ways, to influence system outcomes. These outcomes are called "system patterns," which then guide the way people think, behave, and act, and that produce the overall outcomes of a system. The Grey Zone of Change is relevant because we are living in an age of complexity and emergence (defined further below), where existing systems that guide thoughts, behaviours, and actions are in tension with developing ones. Systems (organizations, social systems, political systems) include ways of organizing/doing and ways of thinking and being (philosophies/worldviews) and they are often interconnected.

Organization Development (OD) *refers to the interdisciplinary field of scholars and practitioners who work collaboratively with organizations and communities to develop their system-wide capacity for effectiveness and vitality. It is grounded in the organization and social sciences.* This definition is the one proposed by a representative working group of scholars and practitioners in the field after a review of 38 variations of OD definitions in the literature. In its simplest form, I use a working definition of OD as the application of the behavioral, organization and social sciences to develop groups of people from where they are to where they want to go through high-engagement and high-inquiry processes (Gilpin-Jackson, 2018).

Since the emergence of OD after the Second World War, there has been much variation in its definition. A 2002 review revealed 27 definitions in the literature (Egan, 2002). In a recent professional working group made up of scholars and internal and external practitioners, 11 more definitions were added to the Egan (2002) list, yielding 38 documented definitions alluded to above, along with my 2018 working one above. Nonetheless, what has been clear to me throughout the review process is that there are core enduring features of OD that hold true for all:

- *Humanistic:* anchored in humanistic values of democracy, participation, informed consent, positive human potential, and thriving.
- *Organization-wide:* focused on an organization-wide shift, such that every level of the organization—individual, groups and the whole—are developed. In its larger human development frame, organization-wide refers to the desired impact of shifting entire communities or social systems.
- *Developmental-focused:* designed to create learning that yields a holistic development shift to higher levels of understanding and maturation.
- *Systems-oriented:* held by OD practitioners in recognition that change and development are impacted by the entire socio-technical system as well as the external environment. Strategy (inclusive of environmental scanning and trend spotting), structure, and culture, plus human and technical systems and processes all coalesce to achieve operational, aspirational, and developmental goals. Thus, OD practitioners uniquely hold a systems perspective to change and development and, from that vantage point, they question the impact of human and technical processes on the performance, effectiveness, and vigour of the organization.
- *Research and evidence-informed:* OD is fundamentally an applied field that privileges understanding organizational contexts through data-gathering to inform forward actions in its diagnostic form as defined below. The founding father of the field, Kurt Lewin, is famously reputed to have said: "No research without action, no action without research" (Marrow, 1969). In the dialogic form of OD as noted below, human experience that arises from language and conversation is valid evidence and is part of change processes.

Diagnostic Organization Development *refers to traditional OD practice in which a formal investigation is conducted so that objective data are collected and analyzed to make a diagnosis and to make recommendations for problem-solving.*

In this original rendition of OD, research is conducted from the perspective that data is an objective, locatable "truth." Concomitantly, if an accurate "diagnosis" can be made, then an expert intervention to fill gaps and correct deficiencies is possible. It is a cause-and-effect orientation which assumes that factors affecting organizational life can be mechanistically manipulated. Examples of Diagnostic OD methodologies are the classic action research and survey feedback processes and any approach grounded in the Kurt Lewin model of change: "unfreeze-change-refreeze" (Lewin, 1947).

Dialogic Organization Development *refers to OD practices and mindset, anchored in an understanding of human systems as socially constructed; every interaction and conversation is part and parcel of creating the change.* Everyone is seen as having part of the "truth" (subjective) which is better understood as shared meaning-making. Every exchange is an intervention into the organization. In the Dialogic OD frame, everything arises in conversation and every interaction is data. Actions and outcomes are co-created through inquiry, not enacted by "experts." The leader (or practitioner) works with the people most impacted by the desired transformation, gives them the freedom and the power to define the change processes, and then manages said processes on behalf of the stakeholders (Bushe, 2020). This, as you can imagine, is easier said than done. Dialogic OD is characterized by the change processes of emergence, generativity, and new narratives, which contribute to the desired transformational change outcomes (Bushe & Marshak, 2015b).

Dialogic Organization Development Mindset *is the orientation from which an individual, practitioner, or leader holds Dialogic OD assumptions and worldviews as their primary mental model for engaging with others. This mindset is present regardless of the methodology being used.* As noted by the proponents of Dialogic OD: "It is important to understand that the Dialogic OD Mindset is a newer orientation to the practice of OD that is not associated with any specific method. There are dozens of methods that can be used dialogically…but many of those methods can also be used diagnostically. It is one's mindset that determines how one thinks about and engages situations, including selecting and mixing which methods and approaches to use" (Bushe & Marshak, 2015c, p. 14). Do you consider every conversation and interaction to be an opportunity for individual and collective change? Do you listen for valid information to influence your thinking, behaviours, and actions? Do you consider your own experience and meaning-making and that of others as valid "data" that influence actions and outcomes? If you are saying "yes" to any of this, you are operating from a dialogic mindset. In this mindset, objective data is useful as a starting point to generate conversation and meaning-making. Subjective experience and interactions are equally valid interventions for change.

Complexity, Disruption, Emergence and Adaptive Actions: *Complexity is the study of chaos and (dis)order. Disruption is a core requirement for entering the Grey Zone of Change, because it is the signal (event(s) or situations) of seismic proportions that fundamentally challenge(s) the status quo and known assumptions.* Disruptions signal that an existing system needs to change and that a new system is emerging. When disruptions happen, the differences within and between agents of a system are amplified; they interact in unpredictable ways until they reorder or self-organize into a new coherence *Emergence is the new order or pattern arising from chaos when an existing pattern or order is disrupted.* However, in a complex world, the way forward is unknown and unpredictable because there are no clear cause-and-effect relationships and no "right" answers. *The way forward lies in continually creating conditions to see, understand, and influence emerging patterns* (Holman, 2010; Human Systems Dynamics Institute, 2020a, Snowden & Boone, 2007). *This cyclical approach to making* *progress in the midst of complexity is called "adaptive action."*

Generativity *refers to the field of possibility, yet unknown, that is evoked or uncovered when the right conversations take place.* It is the new idea(s), image(s) or metaphor(s) that is (are) only sparked when dialogue and conversation happen between people. It is those neurological insights, which we call "Aha!" moments, that occur when people resonate with others' ideas and stories. Marshak describes generative conversations as being "based on the premise that the way people see and respond to the world is determined by out-of-awareness cognitive structures that may not be identified and addressed during everyday conversations" (Marshak, 2004, p.25). Generative conversations uncover the hidden potential in organizations and help people to co-construct richer and deeper transformational change (van den Nieuwenhof, 2013). The dynamics of generative change, and the means by which generativity can be evoked through consulting and coaching conversations, are addressed in detail elsewhere in Bushe (2020) and Marshak (2020).

Narrative Formation: *When an organization is experiencing disruption, there is often a dominant storyline that may be limited in its generativity or may no longer be serving some of its members. As conversations are woven together through Dialogic OD processes, new meanings and stories are formed that help people articulate and make sense of changes and create new narratives.* The formation of a new and coherent narrative is often a signal that new patterns are emerging. The development of shared narratives as part of Dialogic OD processes is essential to how people in organizations accept or reject change as they co-construct and realize transformations (Sonenshein, 2010). *A narrative combines a series of stories and identity conclusions that individuals and groups adopt; it also includes expressive forms such as metaphors, symbols, slogans, imagery, etc.* For example, in a geographically dispersed and mobile work team I led, we engaged in a Dialogic OD process focused on our narrative in the midst of other systemic disruptions we were experiencing. We characterized our experience of chaos and our own team disconnection at the time as "the Scream." We then named the emerging narrative we subsequently amplified over two years as "Living Together, Apart," which became our tagline for the new storyline we were co-creating. This tagline had both the autonomy of the independent practice and flexibility that we wanted to maintain, and the unifying structure of our shared professional practice, values and support that we wanted to call upon as needed. It strikes me that this narrative corresponds to the current reality of our global and virtually connected world.

Transformational Change *refers to a fundamental shift in a system's ways of thinking, doing and being.* Positive transformation is the desired outcome of Dialogic OD processes and most often requires a journey through the Grey Zone of Change. In the ideal case, transformational change also occurs at the individual level, from participating in a process that can result in cognitive and affective changes, and in an overall experiential and worldview shift (Cranton & Taylor, 2012; Gilpin-Jackson, 2015; Kegan, 2000; Marshak, 2002; Yorks & Kasl, 2006).

Development, *as used in this context, refers to a positive shift in understanding, orientation, and overall capacity, such that an organization as an entity is better able to "talk to itself about itself," to address issues proactively versus reactively, and to self-actualize its potential* (Bushe & Nagaishii, 2018).

The Four Sections of this Guidebook

Section 1: *Understanding the Grey Zone of Change* expands upon what the Grey Zone of Change is. I discuss why it will perhaps always be with us, and I unpack its dynamics. I include a discussion of its system dynamics, psychodynamics, and group dynamics and its possible applications for addressing trauma and for inducing positive change.

Section 2: *Navigating the Grey Zone of Change* covers the overall choices, competencies, and mindsets required for living with the grey zone. I then present some considerations for living, leading, and facilitating transformations in the Grey Zone of Change.

Section 3: *Facilitating Transformation in the Grey Zone of Change* proposes a comprehensive framework for working toward transformation within the Grey Zone of Change, encompassing the following Dialogic OD stages: Initiating the Dialogic Inquiry, Facilitating the Dialogic Journey, and Sustaining the Transformation.

Section 4: *Lessons from the Grey Zone of Change*, covers what gets in the way, what helps, and it offers strategies for supporting self and others through the Grey Zone of Change.

Each section ends with a short case or example, further inquiry questions or guidelines, and an application exercise to support leaders and practitioners who are working toward transformation in the Grey Zone of Change.

SECTION 1:

Understanding the Grey Zone of Change

In this section, we will explore the following key questions.

1. What is the Grey Zone of Change?
2. Why the Grey Zone of Change?
3. What are the dynamics of the Grey Zone of Change?
4. What are the impacts of the Grey Zone of Change?

What is the Grey Zone of Change?

I define the Grey Zone of Change as the space in-between an existing system (System A) and an emerging or envisioned one (System B) *that is undefined and unknowable*. By "systems," I mean complex adaptive structures with many interconnected parts, facing novel challenges whose solutions are unknown. For example, an organization may be responding to the need for greater responsiveness in getting products to market by moving into new product development and by changing from hierarchical top-heavy decision-making to decentralized collaborative teams. Its leadership may envision giving delegated decision-making authority during the design and product development phases to these collaborative teams. This type of change is transformational, as it will require a shift in the way people think, work, and interact with each other. It will plunge the organization into a Grey Zone of Change, where three things need to happen before transformation can start to emerge: Transition, Learning & Synthesis, and Group Development. These are the sub-zones within the Grey Zone of Change.

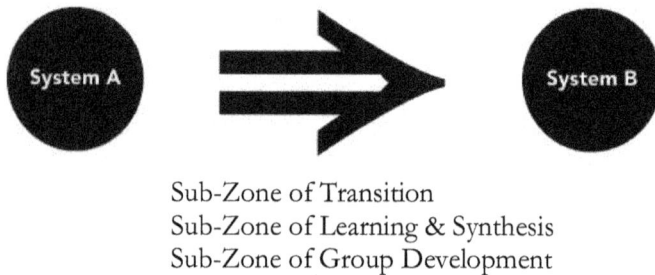

Sub-Zone of Transition
Sub-Zone of Learning & Synthesis
Sub-Zone of Group Development

Figure 1-1: The Grey Zone of Change

The Sub-Zone of Transition
As popularized by William Bridges, change is an event, whereas transition is the individual psychological experience underlying the change event (Bridges, 1991). The transition experience is marked by the ending, the neutral zone, and the new beginning.

The ending allows for articulating what is being lost as well as what is being gained. This is a significant contribution of the Bridges model because losses have often been left out of the conversation in traditional change management. The neutral zone is the zone of sensemaking, with many questions and no "right" answers. It is characterized by chaos, confusion, and a lot of unknowns. It is, however, the realm of much creativity where new possibilities begin to emerge, especially when the environment is conducive to exploration and experimentation. This leads to the new beginning, when the envisioned System B becomes a reality.

Another description of the transition of systems and what is required in the Grey Zone of Change comes from Margaret Wheatley's work on integrating the new science of systems thinking into Leadership and Organization Development (Wheatley, 1994). She co-founded the Berkana Institute, which has worked with communities around the world to scale social innovations. The Berkana Institute developed a two-loop model that summarized the transition zone of the grey zone perfectly (Berkana Institute, 2013). The model articulates three roles: Stabilizers of the old system, Bridge-builders for the transition, and Creators of the new systems. "In brief, as one system peaks and begins to falter, alternatives start to arise in isolation. Slowly, the old collapses and the new arises. The essential work in organizations is to hospice the old, midwife the new, and build bridges between worldviews" (Holman, 2015, p. 134). It is important to consider where you are in the transition process (ending, neutral, or new beginning), and what role you are animating at different points in time (stabilizer, bridge-builder, or creator). Understanding where you are will help you determine your next actions and choices in the Grey Zone of Change.

Transition work helps leaders and change practitioners understand why achieving successful change outcomes takes much longer than the moment at which the ribbon is cut or the technology system is installed. That is because people need to transition, which is essential to working through the grey zone. My favorite personal example concerns the event of birthing my first child and the transition experience of internalizing that I had become a mother. It took me the first year of my daughter's life to understand that how I had lived (my system of life) before her birth was changing into a new system. By the time she was 18 months old and I was expecting my second child, the new beginning was emerging and taking shape. I had accepted the loss of certain freedoms and independence (What?! I have to schedule a meet-up with a girlfriend around baby's naptime?!). I had also gone through the initial confusion and uncertainties of the neutral zone with the realization that there are still many unknowns to parenting (What?! There's no definitive manual for parenting?!). In the midst of that, my husband and I got creative and started figuring out what routines would work for our growing family, so that when my third child came along, I was already operating in the new beginning. We were still learning, but the confusion of the neutral zone had faded away somewhat.

By way of a professional example, I worked with a consulting group where we agreed to shift significantly from a full-scale Organization Development consulting practice to a Leadership Development specialty firm. We also agreed that we would always have co-facilitators on every assignment, for all the wonderful reasons like client relationship management and continuity, knowledge management, and succession. We thought that this would be a simple shift. We were so wrong. The transition took us at least three years before it felt as though we had found our new rhythm as a firm. It took a lot of learning and development, which I will say more about below.

The Sub-Zone of Learning & Synthesis

In the grey zone, much learning needs to happen. The learning sub-zone is the space between not-knowing and knowing. It entails the processes of comprehending what an experience or event actually means. This zone has been described by developmental and learning theorists as encompassing the processes of adaptation, assimilation, and accommodation, or the zone of proximal development. Robert Kegan has called this the "zone of mediation where meaning is made" (Kegan, 1982, p. 2-3). In the grey zone, this meaning-making and synthesis is essential to the learning needed to adapt and move forward. As you will see in Section 3, this learning includes transformative learning as well as instructive learning such as acquiring a new skill, and communicative learning. Communicative learning is how we engage and communicate with each other and is often a part of transformative learning. It is out of the transformative learning that happens individually and collectively that generative change is co-created (Bushe, 2020).

Take for example, the decision mentioned above to shift from a full-scale Organization Development consulting practice to a Leadership Development specialty firm. Once we arrived at a consensus concerning leadership development as our specialty, each of us needed to undergo instructive learning. Some of us needed to learn how to write facilitative guides/instructional manuals, a skill that does not necessarily come with an OD education and background. The transformative learning that was significant was the shift from being an "expert" individual practitioner who was responsible for determining the direction of each client's intervention and design on their own, to being collaborators and co-facilitators. Each of us had to learn how to let go of control and to share space, and we collectively had to learn collaboration skills. We discovered how to learn together. We became very intentional about debriefing after every client delivery—documenting and integrating lessons learned in new ways, and spending endless hours defining and experimenting with what co-facilitation meant for us. This involved individual and collective meaning-making of our co-facilitation experiences. We also learned how to be nimble and to adapt our strategies and ways of working as we figured out what worked well and what didn't.

The learning process required in the grey zone is neither easy nor simple. The Grey

Zone of Change requires us to engage different behaviours than those we had acquired by default. It isn't simply about "letting go" of the old ways in their entirety, but also about "moving forward" with those aspects of the old that could be useful in the new era. It is an interwoven and nested learning and (un)learning process in which new identities are forged BECAUSE of where we have been. This is why working, leading or facilitating in the grey zone takes effort. It requires more mental energy and focused attention than our defaults. It requires us to get out of autopilot. It requires integrating and synthesizing the "old" and "new" ways, not in opposition to one another, but by holding both in the balance and understanding when to emphasize elements of one or the other, when and how to integrate a blended approach where needed, and most importantly, when to let go of elements of either that do not serve the emerging future. It is a dance at the edge of polarity management (Johnson, 1992) that is inevitable as you will see in the following section, Dynamics of the Grey Zone of Change.

For example, a practitioner recently asked me: "How do I create the future we are envisioning and designing while working within old structures?" My response was that they needed to prototype the new and teach themselves and others the required shifts for the emerging future. They needed to do this (un)learning while still functioning within the traditional structures.

The Sub-Zone of Group Development
It is not enough to go through the transition and learning at an individual level. It must happen at a whole system level as well. The collective of people impacted by the transformations at hand need enough shared experience of transitioning and learning together to evolve sufficiently to achieve change. Of course, this is fraught with the complexities and chaos that ensue in the Grey Zone of Change, underscored by issues of leadership, individual engagement, impacts of structure, policy and process changes and human agency/choice as a system moves from disruption to coherence. This is the tough stuff (yes, "tough," not "soft!") that is the make-or-break in whether a collective human system will change. The challenge is that humans transition at different speeds and have different experiences of the same events. This is why collective meaning-making is critical for large-scale transformation and why methodologies that foster collective sensemaking are essential.

By bringing groups together to share their experiences and stories, people are able to see the big picture, to understand each other, and to have an opportunity to generate a new shared narrative together. Otherwise, transition, learning, and synthesis will occur at varying speeds that may not result in collective transformation. This creates the group experience in which a change event has occurred, but people continue to operate as-is, rather than adopt the change.

Dynamics of the Grey Zone of Change

The grey zone is characterized by human experiences that occur in unknown territory where our greatest challenge may be to resolve the anxiety of not knowing. There are three types of dynamics that must be understood to work the grey zone: System Dynamics, Psychodynamics, and Group Dynamics

System Dynamics

For a long time, open systems theory provided a framework for thinking about the way an organization responded to those inputs and feedback from the external environment that determined its outputs. We are now living in a time of complex adaptive systems, which describe much more difficulty than open systems. The definition of complex adaptive systems (CAS), based on the work of Dooley (1997), and offered by the Human Systems Dynamics Institute is "a group of semi-autonomous agents who interact in interdependent ways to produce system-wide patterns, such that those patterns then influence behavior of the agents" (Human Systems Dynamics Institute, 2020b, p.1).

A CAS approach accounts for the reality that while we are interdependent, human behaviour is still unpredictable. Just as in natural systems, human systems will produce patterns that will naturally emerge, whether we intervene to shape them by design or not. This means that it is possible to look for system patterns in the Grey Zone of Change, to seek to understand them, and to influence desired shifts by changing any of the three conditions that determine the speed, direction, and path of a system as it self-organizes. These conditions are the containers, differences, and exchanges of a system (Human Systems Dynamics Institute, 2020c).

Containers are the boundaries that hold a system together while people self-organize for patterns to emerge. Containers may be physical locations or gathering places or they may be conceptual or ideological—like the terms of reference of a steering committee or a political agenda.

Differences are the elements of diversity that exist within systems, including biographical or social markers, professions, personalities, and so on. Too little difference may cause a system to stagnate, while too much difference may create patterns of dysfunction that make it difficult for productive alignment. Creative energy lies within differences, however, and that power must be harnessed for innovation and generativity to emerge.

Exchanges are the means by which information flows within and between systems and their environments. They also encompass how the people in a system interact with one another. Exchanges include conversations, meetings, and all forms of information sharing.

Most often, the impetus for change in a CAS is a disruption. When a system is, or appears to be, at rest or at equilibrium (System A), a disruption sparks disequilibrium. The opportunity opens for people in the system to make meaning of what is happening and to take actions such that new patterns may emerge at another level of coherence (System B). This reorganizing of a system will naturally occur with or without deliberate action of system agents, because of the self-organizing characteristic of a CAS. Essentially, disruptions will keep pushing a system from its equilibrium until the system reaches a bifurcation point, where it either falls into a fragmented state of (in)coherence, or reorganizes into a more developed, differentiated, and coherent CAS.

The opportunity in the grey zone is to notice disruptions and to facilitate in ways that allow generative self-organizing to emerge. An understanding of containers, differences, and exchanges allows leaders and practitioners to see, understand, and influence the emergence of new patterns in the Grey Zone of Change. In Section 3, I discuss the role of leaders and practitioners in watching for and amplifying the patterns that are supportive of change and of positively addressing the complex challenges at hand.

Psychodynamics

The psychodynamics of the grey zone are centered around anxiety. As work on the neuroscience of change has confirmed, anything impacting the status, certainty, autonomy, relatedness, and fairness (SCARF) in human systems will raise anxiety, producing a neurological pain response equal to that of physical pain. This triggers our survival instincts (Rock & Schwartz, 2006; Rock, 2008). The result is that the Grey Zone of Change is fraught with anxiety by all human agents in a system—clients, leaders, consultants, individual contributors, groups, and networks—who will all be triggered and who will all want to reduce or eliminate anxiety and restore order. This presents challenges and unique opportunities for navigating the Grey Zone of Change as will be discussed further in Section 2.

Group Dynamics

Just as individual psychodynamics are at play in the Grey Zone of Change, so too are group dynamics. By group, I am referring here to people in a human system with a shared purpose. The group as the unit of analysis in the grey zone could be a small group, a large group, an organization, or some other social system. Group Dynamics are the patterns that impact the overall functioning of a group, the patterns that emerge according to how its members interact and work together. I believe that the fundamentals of group life and group dynamics are often forgotten when attempting to enact a change, which is a major reason that transformational outcomes are often delayed. Think, for example, about times when you have been part of a group change that has taken longer than you believe was necessary, because issues were swept under the table or unresolved. More often than not, those issues were related to group dynamics. This aspect of OD practice can be underemphasized and underdeveloped when a more diagnostic form of educating and developing people for supporting transformations is employed. This is because group dynamics cannot be predetermined or planned. They emerge as change processes and conversations unfold and they need to be understood, discussed, and integrated as they emerge. Working with group dynamics, however, requires practice and skill; when that has not been considered, people may default to what they know, in the hope that the plans will work and the dysfunctional dynamics will go away. As you have likely experienced, this rarely, if ever, works out.

Group dynamics emerge from the fundamental group functions of boundary management (who's in and who's out), task accomplishment (clear agendas), and interpersonal and group management (members' relationships). To perform well, each of these require clear group process and structure (Schein, 2006). As in system dynamics, these functions and related processes and structures form the containers, differences, and exchanges that help groups perform. How well these group functions are operating is quickly visible through the quality of problem-solving, conflict resolution, and members' involvement and interaction.

As indicated earlier, a well-functioning group develops the capacity to talk to itself about itself. Highly developed groups are able to notice and name patterns of dysfunction that no longer serve them and to work together to renew themselves. Less developed groups may have escalated conflict, low performance, and dysfunctional problem-solving and decision-making. In the Grey Zone of Change, groups that struggle with their functioning are likely to experience increased dysfunction due to the chaos and complexity that gets layered on top of the group context. The classic group dysfunctions of Dependency (think unhealthy parent-child attachments), Fight or Flight (think conflict avoidance or conflict escalation) and Pairing (think sub-interest groups and coalitions) may emerge (Bion, 1961). If unaddressed, this can escalate to Trauma (Hopper, 2003, 2012).

Organizational trauma *is the experience of stuckness, paralysis, and hyper-reactivity, felt within the collective as a result of threat(s) to group identity. Organizational trauma reduces individual and organizational performance and creates group dysfunctions.* (Gilpin-Jackson, In-Press). Groups in the grey zone must build the capacity to learn and develop in order to successfully transition to the emerging system. This includes designing group processes to ensure healthy dynamics and attending to any unhealthy patterns as they emerge in the Grey Zone of Change. This is integral to ensuring that groups do not get stuck and move into system decline instead of accomplishing the desired transformation.

Impacts of the Grey Zone of Change

Based on the dynamics discussed above, people and groups in the grey zone are likely to be exposed to the default dysfunctions born of individual anxiety and the group dynamics that unfold when processes are not well-structured.

On the other hand, the grey zone is an open field of possibility. Disruptions often present signals for positive change, which a group humming along in its comfort zone may otherwise miss. When awakened by the disturbance of a disruption, a group ushered into the grey zone has the opportunity to examine what is possible for their individual, group, and cultural formation as they generate new narratives for themselves. The grey zone is an open field for learning & synthesis where creative opportunities for negotiating and designing the future are endless. The possibilities of the grey zone are limited only by the will of individuals and groups and by the mental containers of entrenched past behaviours, which are sometimes difficult to shed. However, groups in the Grey Zone of Change have the opportunity to amplify their positive potentials if they so choose.

Table 1-1 summarizes the elements of the Grey Zone of Change. It shows the sub-zones, the related dynamics within the sub-zones, and possible actions or interventions to ensure understanding at all levels of the human system (personal, group, and whole).

Table 1-1: Elements of the Grey Zone of Change

Elements of the Grey Zone of Change			
Level of the Human system	**Sub-zones**	**Dynamics**	**Possible Interventions**
Personal	• Transition • Learning & Synthesis	• Psychodynamics	• Personal transition sessions • Psychometric assessments • Transformational leadership & learning
Group	• Group Development	• Systems dynamics • Group dynamics	• Interpersonal skills development • Group effectiveness sessions • Whole system design methodologies
System (sustaining the new system)	• Learning & Synthesis • Group Development	• Psychodynamics • Systems dynamics • Group dynamics	• Ongoing learning & synthesis (debriefs, experiential learning) • Integrating new learning/ shifts required to maintain the context of the new system. • Whole system design methodologies

Note that the possible interventions include both Dialogic OD (e.g. whole system methodologies) and Diagnostic OD (e.g. psychometric assessment) practices. The distinguishing factor for success in the grey zone is a Dialogic OD mindset, regardless of the type of practice being used. Further, the specifics of each of the interventions will depend on the details and the context of the particular grey zone situation and on what needs to be amplified for success in your situation. The case described in the next section shows an example of how this might work.

Case-In-Point

In a hospital build and move that I described in a previous publication (Gilpin-Jackson, 2016), the leaders and practitioners were clear about two things. First, they were clear that this was a transformational change opportunity that required leaders at all levels to model transformational leadership. Second, it was a complex situation with many unknowns that would require everyone involved to engage in designing and sustaining the future. In essence, it was a Grey Zone Change. Their goal was to create an extraordinary workplace, where leaders led by example and all stakeholders were engaged in designing and implementing changes to yield desired results. The result was a transformational change that was deemed a resounding success. The move happened on time (actually, 90 mins early), on budget, with clinical services staffed and ready to receive patients. Furthermore, the leadership and collective group engagement and development goals were met.

When looking at this case through the lens of grey zone thinking, it is apparent that the change processes were designed to address all elements of the Grey Zone of Change at every level of the system. Table 1-2 above shows the specific interventions that were used in this case.

They designed two pillars for the change process. One pillar was a series of transformational leadership development sessions for all formal and informal leaders. It entailed core transformational leadership skills such as the ability to recognize one's own narratives, triggers, and entrenched beliefs that can get in the way of relationships and collaboration, along with the Dialogic OD mindset required to lead in the Grey Zone of Change. The second pillar was a series of Conference Model planning sessions for all stakeholders. These dialogically-oriented sessions included a vision conference, a transition conference, and a series of strategic design conferences (Axelrod & Axelrod, 2006). When the design components were aligned across the elements of the Grey Zone of Change, as shown in Table 1-2, every sub-zone was integrated into the design to ensure that transition, learning & synthesis, and group development occurred throughout.

Elements of the Grey Zone of Change in a Hospital Build and Move			
Level of the Human system	**Sub-zones**	**Dynamics**	**Interventions in a Hospital Build and Move Case**
Personal	• Transition • Learning & Synthesis	• Psychodynamics	• A transition conference. • Transformational leadership development sessions for all formal and informal leaders focused on transforming personal patterns that get in the way of leading change effectively with intentional application to the challenges and opportunities they were facing. • Learning fairs to build and spread skills needed for success.
Group	• Group Development	• Systems dynamics • Group dynamics	• Vision, customer and design conferences. • Intentional walkthroughs (sharing of conference outputs with those who did not attend) to ensure different voices were heard and perspectives integrated. • Intentional space for group dialogue about emerging group patterns within conferences.
Whole System (sustaining the new system)	• Learning & Synthesis • Group Development	• Psychodynamics • Systems dynamics • Group dynamics	• Debrief sessions (with planners, leaders & sponsors) to capture & synthesize learnings to carry forward after conferences. • Self-organized action groups working on identified priorities and testing various actions to see what might work. • All applying insights from their learnings in the conferences and transformational leadership sessions within their action groups and areas of work.

Table 1-2: Designing for Elements of the Grey Zone of Change

Here is a quote from one stakeholder that shows some of the dynamics experienced, and some of the ways in which the grey zone sub-zones were addressed and experienced by participants through the design:

> …you know now that I think back, it could've been so traumatic and it really wasn't. I just have fond memories of the transition and the excitements around it all and for me I think it was the conferences…or what came out of the conferences… being able to talk, you know, share with each other what kind of things could be done to commemorate the old, remember the old and what kind of things to bring along. (quoted in Gilpin-Jackson, 2016, p. 425)

In analyzing this case, I concluded that **Transformational experiences (TE)** *in Large-Scale Organization Development Interventions are a function of* **contextual conditions (C)**, **personal transformation (tP)** *and* **organizational transformation (tO)**, *where contextual conditions have a multiplier effect on the attainment of transformation.* TE = C [tP + tO]. In simple terms, both personal (leadership) and whole group (organizational or other) transformation are required for successful organizational transformation. However, the "container" of the change must also have the conditions that support transformation. In other words, if people and/or the organization transform(s), but the environment they live in does not support the transformation, change will be short-lived. In the hospital case, the focus on transformational leadership at every level of the organization was intended to create leadership capacity for the future and to create the container for success. The formula provides a guide for designing interventions to ensure that the personal and group elements of the sub-zones and the dynamics of the grey zone are attended to. Further discussion of how this formula may guide design of change processes in the grey zone is provided in Section 3.

Core Questions & Guidelines: Understanding the Grey Zone

Here are 10 questions that may guide you in understanding and responding to the immediate experiences of the Grey Zone of Change:

1. How am I/we experiencing the three sub-zones (transition, learning & synthesis, and group development) of the Grey Zone of Change?
    o What are the current transition experiences? (Are those involved predominantly in the ending zone (feelings of loss & stuck emotional responses), neutral zone (confusion and creativity) or new beginning (already operating at new normal)?
    o What am I/we already learning/synthesizing in relation to the change?
    o What is the level of group development I am experiencing?
        ▪ A) We are underdeveloped (unable to talk and plan together for the critical aspects of the change)

- - B) We are somewhat developed (able to talk and plan together for some but not all of the critical aspects of the change)
  - C) We are developing through this change together (able to talk and plan together for most of the critical aspects of the change)
2. What transition role am I currently fulfilling: stabilizer of the old system, bridge-builder between the old and new systems, or creator of the new system?
3. What do I/we stand to lose?
4. What do I/we stand to gain?
5. What questions, if answered, will move us forward?
6. What elements of the "old" culture need to be carried into the "new?"
7. How do I/we need to develop in order to be prepared for what is emerging?
8. What containers (boundaries that hold a system together), differences (elements of diversity that exist within systems) and/or exchanges (information flows within and between systems) do I/we need to influence?
9. How might I/we manage our anxiety and reactivity in the grey zone in order to achieve transformation?
10. What (un)learning needs to happen for me, for the group, and for the entire system to sustain success?

Some guidelines to consider to help you and/or your group understand your Grey Zone of Change experience or situation include:

1. Create a wall/floor chart of the transition experiences by mapping your assessment of where you think people might be and then asking people where they place themselves.
   a. Are they involved predominantly in the ending zone (feelings of loss & stuck emotional responses), neutral zone (confusion and creativity) or new beginning (already operating at new normal)?). Discuss any discrepancies and help people think through options for helping people through the transition journey.
   b. Assess what roles people are exhibiting and determine which role(s) you may need to introduce to support further progress.
      i. Stabilizers—maintaining the stability of the "old" system.
      ii. Bridge-builders—helping shepherd people from the old to the emerging future.
      iii. Creators—Designing the "new" system.
2. Determine the best mechanism to help you and the group reflect and synthesize what you are learning in the grey zone. This may include any form of debriefing, checking-in on lessons learned, and/or open discussions of failures and what needs to be unlearned.
3. Create space to examine your group processes of communication, decision-making, member commitment to action, and anything else that might be

relevant to the group's effective functioning through the grey zone. This will enable the group to develop together as well as to work on its dynamics.

4. Attend to anxiety and promote a non-anxious presence. Note it, normalize it and model it. This will be harder for those with higher needs for certainty, clarity, and planning. Psychometric assessments can help people understand themselves and others and to interact with empathy and support for each other.

5. Use an understanding of systems dynamics (containers, differences, and exchanges) to uncover, understand, and influence patterns that are stuck and need to be shifted, and patterns that are working and can be amplified. *How well are our current containers serving us? What new containers might we need? How well are our current differences serving us? What differences might we need to introduce? How well are our current exchanges serving us? What new exchanges might we need to create?* Encourage people and groups to self-organize to experiment with a variety of ways to shift or amplify patterns based on their responses to these questions.

Summary

The Grey Zone of Change is the space in between an existing system (System A) and an emerging or envisioned one (System B) *that is undefined and unknowable.* In the grey zone, three things need to happen before transformation can start to emerge: Transition, Learning, and Group Development. I call these the sub-zones within the Grey Zone of Change.

The net effect of a system that has transitioned, learned well, and developed together is transformation. It is a new state in which how the collective thinks and acts is fundamentally and qualitatively different than before.

Leaders and practitioners working to achieve transformational change must understand the individual, group, and systems dynamics needed to achieve transformation. They must create the conditions for individual, group, and collective transition and development. Navigating the grey zone to achieve all of this—not simply a successful change event or short-term behaviour change—is required. A Dialogic Organization Development mindset makes it possible for leaders and practitioners to navigate the complexity of the grey zone, and is expanded on in Sections 2 and 3. Diagnostic orientations also have a place in the grey zone in providing frameworks for tracking beginning and end states, measuring progress, managing incremental changes, and tracking the evolution and development of the system.

Application

1. Create a list of grey zone experiences you are currently involved in – personally, professionally and socially.

2. For each of the grey zone experiences, assess, discuss with others, and make notes on the following. Note concrete observations/examples.
    a. What patterns are emerging in the grey zone?
    b. What psychodynamics—psychosocial, emotional, and mental impacts—are you experiencing?
    c. What group dynamics are you observing?
    d. What is your current experience of the impacts of each of the grey zones?
    e. What new insights have you gained by using these ideas to understand your grey zone experiences?

3. Brainstorm a list of actions that could help you create the Grey Zone of Change experience you want. Choose one that you will try immediately.

SECTION 2

Navigating the Grey Zone of Change

In this section, we'll explore the following key questions.

1. What are the choices in the Grey Zone of Change?
2. What overall qualities and mindsets are required for navigating the Grey Zone of Change?
3. How can you navigate the Grey Zone of Change as an individual?
4. What qualities do you need to lead effectively in the Grey Zone of Change?
5. What qualities do you need as a consultant/facilitator in the Grey Zone of Change?

Choices in the Grey Zone of Change

There are three response choices for navigating the Grey Zone of Change when disruptions signal a system in need of transformation. Such disruptions may be anything that potentially changes the fundamental way people work when they are in the equilibrium of their comfort zone. Therefore, a disruption is anything that creates disequilibrium in the status quo, because it presents a threat. For example, a new technology, a new market competitor, internal changes (e.g. employees decide to unionize). People in a system can decide to:

1. respond to the disturbance reactively.
2. maintain the status quo.
3. respond to the disturbance proactively.

In the first choice, leaders and people involved may be spending most of their time reacting to the increased disorder and disequilibrium of the Grey Zone of Change as disruptions escalate. This is a situation where people are working in crisis management mode, "fixing" issues as they arise. This may be an unconscious choice, where disorder is seen as inevitable and par for the course. It also means exhibiting reactive behaviours in which people are operating in survival fight or flight mode. In fight mode, people may act defensively or offensively to protect their territory. In flight mode, people may be in denial or ignore the disruptions because they are resigned or feel powerless to make substantive changes. In this way of navigating the grey zone, reacting to what shows up is seen as THE job. Indeed, in this world, leaders are rewarded for their exceptional "fire-fighting" skills. Crisis management is the norm. Stress levels tend to be high and people tend to move from one crisis to the next. This way of working and being may well become part of the new way as the system reorganizes itself to new levels of (in)coherence and (dis)equilibrium. Although it may be argued that this form of working is inevitable in certain industries such as emergency response, a proactive engagement strategy and response choice is always possible even in these contexts, as elaborated on in the discussion of the third response choice.

The second response choice is one in which people consciously or unconsciously work to maintain the status quo. Here, people either actively work to keep things "the way they have always been," or espouse alignment with the transformational change possibilities while holding competing commitments that maintain the status quo (Kegan & Lahey, 2001). This is the response choice in which people are seen as "resisting change."

In my view, people do not resist change, they resist HOW change occurs. In general, people "resist" autocratic change processes where they are not engaged in decisions that impact them (Axelrod, 2011; Kim & Mauborgne, 2003), and where they may stand to lose what has become familiar. As neuroscience has confirmed, survival instincts are triggered when change announcements and processes occur as threats to people's status, certainty, autonomy, relatedness, and sense of fairness SCARF (Rock, 2008) Therefore, people may choose to actively keep things as they are, within their comfort zone, seeking to avoid any threat or anxiety.

A Dialogic OD mindset is key to the capacity to engage the disruption signals of the grey zone proactively, as recommended in the third response choice. One way to inspire this mindset in situations in which a status-quo mentality seems to be predominant is to redefine resistance. A Dialogic OD mindset allows for an appreciative lens to amplify the benefits of the roles people bring to transformation that may be otherwise labelled as "resistance." For example, people considered traditionalists, who bring order and structure, may be seen as stabilizers who, when engaged appropriately, bring order to the chaos and help create structures to accelerate the emergence of a new system balance. Sensors are seen as advocates for a variety of perspectives. Frame-setters are focused on identity and direction, and innovators inspire change and host the conversations needed to help the system get unstuck (Roehrig, Schwendenwein, & Bushe, 2015). These can be categorized within the three main transition roles offered in Section 1: Stabilizers, Bridge-builders, and Creators.

The third response choice is to engage disruptions proactively by anticipating and leading the future. This entails scanning the internal and external environment to spot signals of disruption and of emerging patterns that will impact a system early. It means being in inquiry about what signals mean, and proactively testing out system innovations and new patterns of interactions to get feedback on what is occurring as the system seeks to differentiate and find new coherence. This is a proactive and conscious choice. It is possible in all contexts including emergency response environments. For example, a number of organizations in healthcare and other high-risk environments such as aviation are taking on the strategy of high-reliability organizations (HROs), which is "a subset of hazardous organizations that enjoy a high level of safety over long periods of time" (Stralen, 2011).

Characteristics of HROs include: (1) prioritizing safety and performance as organizational goals, (2) a culture of reliability with de-centralized decision-making, (3) a learning response to accidents, incidents and near-misses, and (4) a strategy of redundancy in technology as well as people. This allows HROs and other proactive organizations to be constantly scanning systems and strategically orienting to the future. These organizations impact markets and the economy. As they lead systems change, they become disruptors to the world around them. Think about organizations such as Apple, Mastercard, GE, Nike, and others who are leading the global grey zone by being the first to market technologies and services that are changing the world as we navigate our fourth industrial revolution (*Fortune* magazine, 2019).

Engaging emergence proactively is the ideal approach to navigating the Grey Zone of Change. As indicated earlier, systems will reorganize themselves following disruptions whether they engage proactively or not. However, it is important to know which context you are working within. You may be in an industry or organization that is deliberately taking a lag (reactive) strategy over a lead (proactive) strategy. In that case, continuing to push for a proactive approach may either be welcomed as innovative or rejected as an unnecessary disturbance. It is important as a starting point to navigating the Grey Zone of Change to get clear on:

- ☐ What response strategy is my preference in the Grey Zone of Change? (reactive, status-quo or proactive)
- ☐ What is my organization's orientation to navigating the Grey Zone of Change?
- ☐ What response choice do I want to be operating in?
- ☐ What will it take for me to effectively navigate the Grey Zone of Change proactively?

Mindsets & Shifts for Navigating the Grey Zone of Change

The approach I have found to effectively and proactively navigate the Grey Zone of Change is a Dialogic OD mindset. The Dialogic OD mindset is best suited to achieving transformational change. It is anchored in the philosophy and ideals of social constructivism—that change is emergent and happens in every interaction—regardless of which OD or other methodology is being utilized. For example, Table 2-1 presents a summary of how the Grey Zone of Change is positioned relative to the ideals of Diagnostic and Dialogic OD. It shows, for example, that the Grey Zone of Change requires blended use of all three generations of OD methodologies. Expertise is required in first-generation (diagnostic), second-generation (action learning) and third generation (dialogic) methodologies in the Grey Zone of Change. As I note in the original grey zone case study:

> The art of mastering the grey zone in between diagnostic and dialogic OD becomes how well a practitioner can move along the continuum as appropriate to the circumstance. The crucial element becomes the practitioners' ability to understand the orientations, philosophical bases and intentions of the different forms of OD, such that they can effectively move between and switch their own mental models to practice effectively in either realm. This is not just a question of acquiring diagnostic or dialogic OD skills, but a matter of mastery such that practitioners can safely and effectively practice along the continuum. (Gilpin-Jackson, 2013, p. 62)

Table 2-1: Practicing in the Grey Zone of the Diagnostic to Dialogic OD Continuum. First printed in Organization Development Practitioner 45(1)

	Conventional Diagnostic OD	The Grey Zone	Conventional Dialogic OD
Type of OD Methodologies*	First-generation OD methodologies e.g. action research.	First, second or third generation OD methodologies. Second-generation methodologies include features of Diagnostic & Dialogic OD.	Third-generation OD methodologies, e.g. Appreciative Inquiry.
Goal of OD program, process, approach or inquiry**	Prescriptive diagnosis based on a biological metaphor of organizations. A focus on an ideal identified outcome.	A blend of diagnosis and dialogue as needed at different stages of the change process. A focus on effective change process to realize identified outcomes as well as potential ones.	Emergent self-organizing around a shared vision created in conversation and interaction. A focus on acting on opportunities and potential in the organization system.
Type of OD practice***	Methodology-centred where *diagnostic methods* define the OD program.	Holistic and adaptive practice that is responsive to emergent needs.	Methodology-centred where *dialogic methods* define the OD program.
Philosophical orientation to practice	Knowledge can be objectively discerned through research.	Knowledge is co-created through objective data and emergent subjective realities during the process.	Knowledge is emergent and constructed from real-time social interactions.
Role of OD Practitioner	Expert consultant.	An expert, collaborator, project member, facilitator, trainer, mediator and other roles as situations demand.	Facilitator who recognizes that their presence influences knowledge creation.
Source of OD Interventions****	Interventions are recommended by the OD practitioner.	A blend of the practitioner's expert recommendations and self-organized solutions from organization members.	Interventions are co-created by all involved and especially through self-organizing.
Practitioner influence on implementation	Zero/limited influence where practitioners' role is limited to diagnosis or maximum influence where contracted to implement recommendations.	High influence at early stages where the emphasis is on diagnosis and zero to limited influence as the focus shifts to Dialogic OD.	Zero/limited influence – interventions are implemented through self-organization of participants.

*OD methodologies are the methods, tools, techniques or defined processes used to inquire and/or take actions to improve an organization's effectiveness.

**OD program is a full cycle of research and actions taken to improve organization effectiveness.

***OD Practice is the professional exercise of organizational development using a variety of OD methodologies.

****OD Interventions are the action(s) and methodologies within an OD program.

A recent study corroborated the blended nature and synthesis of methodologies in practice that make up the Dialogic OD mindset. The aim of the study was to explore how leaders and practitioners in Brazil who engaged in Dialogic OD processes understood and described the key premises of their experience and work. The language and metaphors used by participants showed the co-existence of both Diagnostic and Dialogic OD thinking. The authors stated that:

> …because we live in multiple contexts, different traditions come into contact, opening up possibilities for new meanings to be co-created, which then exert force for transformation. In this sense, the results of the study can be related to the Dialogic OD mindset's key premises, revealing that the emergent field of Dialogic OD has been developing in tensional ways, as meanings used by participants to describe their practices exert forces for stability and transformation at the same time…It is therefore important to recognize that, at this moment, the concept of bounded individuals, constructed and rooted over centuries still has a strong influence. So both ideas (Diagnostic and Dialogic OD) may shape the activities of practitioners for a long time in tensional ways. As subject-object dualism persists in the practice of dialogical OD, to be aware of such dualism can turn practices into a more realistic, reflexive, and coherent approach. (Aguiar & Tonelli, 2018, pp. 471-473)

So, what are the shifts required to work, lead or facilitate in the Grey Zone of Change given the blended mastery and ambidexterity required? Given that the outcome of working through the grey zone is transformational change, fundamental shifts are required in *how we think*, *what we do,* and *who we are* in organizations.

Here are some of the core required shifts that matter:

From Hierarchical to Distributed leadership: Everyone in the grey zone needs to contribute ideas and leadership to unfolding changes. This requires a mindset of distributed leadership. Formal leaders must be willing to give up control and informal leaders throughout the system must accept delegated power—authentic permission to innovate, experiment, make mistakes, and learn in the pursuit of what's needed in the new world. In this frame, formal leaders become conveners of a network of informal leaders rather than sole holders of all power and authority.

From Either/Or to Both/And Thinking: In the space between systems, everyone needs to be open to holding polarities in the balance. To do this, people need to be able to let go of deeply held beliefs about the way things are and focus on the way things are becoming…and be willing to have the conversations needed as part of the journey. Self-interest and protecting turf need to be replaced with openness to collective impact. In this frame, all contributors will require learner mindsets over fixed expert mindsets and will need to become capable of letting go of turf in favour of discovering new possibilities.

From Singular Intelligence to Complexity Intelligence: In the grey zone, complexity abounds. Not only might there be multiple polarities to make sense of and continual new factors to contend with, but there may also be patterns emerging that need to be understood and shifted or amplified. Work is built around pattern logic and adaptive action. The capacity to influence patterns through inquiry, coaching, and leading by example becomes paramount.

From Siloed work to Collaborative work: If it were simple to move between systems, any silo could flip the switch and make it happen. The reality is that in the grey zone, no single person or organization has the answer(s), and discerning the way forward requires co-creation with networked partnerships. What's different in this frame is that planning, design, and implementation all happen in open, safe, and diverse spaces, as opposed to closed-door, singularly-oriented spaces. This allows for people to share their anxieties, have their questions answered, learn together—and most importantly, dream together. In this frame, specialists trade their expertise to become knowledge curators and co-creators.

From Fixed Plans to Agility: In the grey zone, fixed plans provide certainty of direction but only have practical utility in helping co-creators find the way forward. What's different in an agility approach is that everyone must learn to adapt as quickly as it becomes clear that planned changes need to be adjusted to incorporate a perspective missed, misunderstood, or even overhauled. Planning is fluid and, in this frame, flexibility is the norm.

From Expert to Learner: In the grey zone, learning through inquiry is all there is. Inquiry is the foundation of social constructivism and the Dialogic OD mindset. The ability to ask the right question(s) and to encourage new possibilities is central to meaning-making, to understanding various perspectives, and to fostering generativity. This requires learning how to (un)learn. It also requires a strong grasp of inquiry and coaching skills, as we will see below.

From Object to Agent/Actor: In addition to all of these shifts that change how we think, what we do, and who we are, one quality continues to be paramount in my experience of working with leaders, groups, organizations, and communities in the grey zone. It has shown up in the leader who has stood up among the gurus to say: "I may be younger but…" It is evident in the person with the unpopular view who insists on speaking up for a perspective that is not being addressed. It is unmistakable in the leader about to retire who stays to contribute to co-creating the vision for a new initiative that they will not see come to fruition because "it will matter to the next generation." That quality is courage—the courage to move from living in the shadows to living in the light. In the shadows, people are getting by, doing what they are told, not speaking up for what matters, and not accountable to seeing things to the end. In the light, people choose courage over fear, which for me is the capacity to use one's voice, to find the strength to act, and to build tenacity. We need to be agents/actors in our world. The chaos and complexity of the grey zone requires that of us. The possibilities and imperatives of our world compel us to act with courage to design the futures we want.

Navigating the Grey Zone: Individuals

As individuals in the Grey Zone of Change, self-care is paramount. The impacts of the shifts needed in the Grey Zone of Change require a lot of us. Acting on what matters to us takes energy, effort and lots of learning. It is a commitment to being in integrity with humanistic values and to upholding the ideals that have long been ascribed to OD, such as democratic values, valid information, free and informed consent, intrinsic commitment, engagement, inquiry, learning, and compassion (Schwarz, 2002). The challenge for individuals in the Grey Zone of Change is to choose this quality of personal commitment and leadership in the midst of the anxiety of the Grey Zone of Change and to balance it with self-care.

In her most recent book, Margaret Wheatly (2017) makes a call to lead and to self-care by creating "islands of sanity" in a world system and civilization that appears to be in collapse. Each of us must ask what this means for us and what version of personal or everyday leadership we will stand for. How will we ensure we do not burn out as we take on proactively engaging the current socio-political and economic/business disturbances facing our world and organizations? What daily choices will we make? What courage is required of us in the places and spaces where we lead? I believe it is the pressures of our times and of living in the grey zone that is making resiliency and self-care the current buzz words, even as the everyday demands of our modern lives escalate (Kegan, 1994). Our mental health and self-care as individuals and as a society have never been more tenuous or more important.

Navigating the Grey Zone of Change: Leaders

The leader's challenge in navigating the Grey Zone of Change is fostering the conditions to define the way forward and to be a partner in making that happen, as opposed to being the architect and owner of the change effort. It is the challenge of upholding high-engagement and inquiry values—basically holding a Dialogic OD mindset. It requires supporting stakeholders to design and define the changes, such that the leader's role is mainly getting implementation obstacles out of the way. Gervase Bushe has shown that leaders who set the conditions for emergence and generativity identify the adaptive challenge, reframe the challenge into a purpose statement, engage diverse stakeholders in generative conversations, stimulate self-organized innovations, learn from successes and failures, and amplify the successes (Bushe, 2019, 2020; Marshak, 2004; Marshak, 2020; van den Nieuwenhof, 2013). The core challenge of this is giving up control and leading by the logic of attraction.

Giving up control is easier said than done but it is a requirement of leading in the Grey Zone of Change. The leader must not only espouse to engage stakeholders in defining change, but must act in consistent ways to build trust, promote fairness in decision-making, and support the agreed-upon processes. Any breach of integrity requires significant trust repair; consistent breakdown between espoused and actual actions will create disengagement (Axelrod, 2011). In this frame of mind, leaders must believe in involving others, not just as an item on a checklist, but as a way of getting things done through intrinsic commitment. It requires leaders to practice the art of inviting others in ways that are compelling enough to enroll them in change vision and action. This is achieved through authentic engagement and sharing what is important to them, while at the same time seeking to understand what is important to stakeholders (Axelrod, 2008; Axelrod, Axelrod, Beedon, & Jacobs, 2004). Shared goals that support transformational change can emerge where the areas of shared importance intersect. Giving up control is essentially about sharing power, fostering communities for action, and knowing when to intervene to exercise decision-making authority effectively.

Leaders who foster conditions for emergence and generativity lead by the logic of attraction as opposed to the logic of replacement. The logic of attraction departs from the logic of replacement with its:

> …focus on moral power, the attractiveness or being state of the change agent, the freedom of the change target, and the role of choice in the transformational process. Kotter asks the question, is change something one manages or something one leads? To manage change is to tell people what to do (a logic of replacement), but to lead change is to show people how to be (a logic of attraction). R.E. Quinn argues that most top managers assume that change is something that someone with authority does to someone who does not have authority. They overlook the logic of attraction and its power to pull change. To engage this logic of attraction, leaders must first make deep changes in themselves, including self-empowerment. When deep personal change occurs,

leaders then behave differently toward their direct reports, and the new behaviours in leaders then attract new behaviours from followers. When leaders model personal change, organizational change is more likely to take place. (Weick & Quinn, 1999, p. 380)

It is clear from this that the leader's work in the Grey Zone of Change is one of deep commitment to self-development and transformational leadership practices which underlie generative leadership.

There are many transformational leadership frameworks, but the practices that I ascribe to, specifically for leading change in unknown territories, are the Deep Change Leadership Practices, described in *Building the bridge as you walk on it: A guide for leading change* (Quinn, 2004). The practices define what Quinn calls the Fundamental State of Leadership. They align with leading in the Grey Zone of Change because this leadership model acknowledges the leader's role in transformation, complexity, and emergence. The fundamental state of leadership entails a commitment to an open and co-creative leadership approach over the traditional command and control leadership approach of maintaining status quo and order. The practices of the Fundamental State of Leadership, listed below, also hold the tensions and polarities of the grey zone:

1. Reflective Action: active and engaged while also mindful and reflective.

2. Authentic Engagement: both principled and engaged "in the game" versus being "on the sidelines."

3. Appreciative Inquiry: seeking the best possibilities in the midst of current reality.

4. Grounded Vision: both grounded in current reality and visionary, looking to the future.

5. Adaptive Confidence: adaptable and flexible while also being confident and secure.

6. Detached Interdependence: Combining independence and strength with humility and openness.

7. Responsible Freedom: spontaneous and flexible while being self-disciplined and responsible.

8. Tough Love: Assertive and bold while also compassionate and concerned.

The Grey Zone of Change is the perfect incubator for practicing transformational leadership, because it attracts people to change and to create the conditions for generativity. It is leadership that supports people to own, define, and design the changes.

It must be noted that the leaders' commitment to transformation and generativity must be matched with equally strong support by a change practitioner, when one is involved as described below. It must also be matched with healthy and generative group dynamics. This comprehensive view is shown in the framework in Section 3. A leader can also achieve transformation with a group by assuming the Dialogic OD consulting functions of the change practitioner. In that case, the leader takes on the role of the facilitative leader who both participates in the content and substance of the changes and supports the group processes (Schwarz, 2002; 2006). While I believe this is a skillset that leaders must have anyway, I also advocate strongly for leaders to know when they can hold this role and when to call in the partnership of a change practitioner. As seen below, incorporating change functions into the leadership role is additive and increases the complexity and challenge for the leader.

Navigating the Grey Zone of Change: Practitioners

In this context, I am referring specifically to internal or external change practitioners who operate from a Dialogic OD mindset. Change practitioners may have the hardest job in the Grey Zone of Change. This is because they hold the cumulative and nested roles of navigating through it first as an individual, second as an informal leader who models the behaviours and values being requested of others, and third as a change practitioner (trusted advisor, consultant, coach, and supporter) to formal leaders. As a change practitioner, you must maintain boundaries and differentiation so that stakeholders experience you as a credible partner, not simply as a colluder or harbinger for the change being fostered by leaders and/or sponsors.

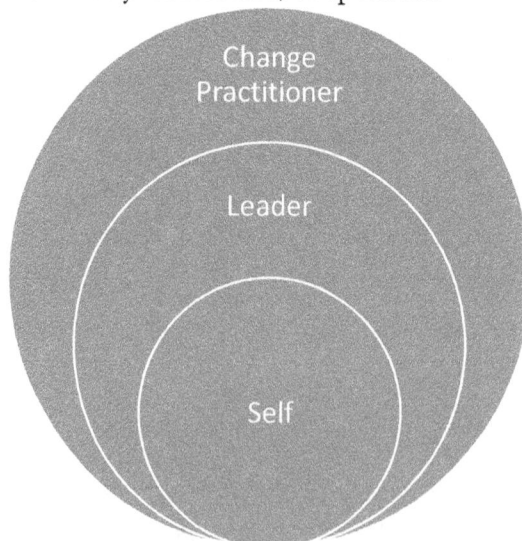

Figure 2-1: Nested roles of a Grey Zone Change Practitioner

This role is both tenuous and powerful. The change practitioner is seemingly powerless with no decision-making or directive authority over stakeholders, bringing nondirective group/change theory, process subject-matter expertise, and a Dialogic OD Mindset. At the same time, the change practitioner is powerful—by being the container, buffer, and throughway for everyone involved. Leaders, sponsors, and stakeholders seek thought partnership and opinions from change practitioners. Thus, change practitioners become the container for the change, holding the knowledge and experience of all sides. They provide coaching and perspective, de-escalating anxieties by being a stabilizing force. They can filter the inputs of all, simply by what they question or do not question, by what they note or do not note on flipcharts, and by how they translate between and within the parties to the change. The ideal in the Grey Zone of Change is that practitioners are doing all of this in a skilled and conscious way with:

1. A Dialogic OD Mindset
2. Masterful Dialogic OD Consulting
3. Self-as-instrument

As introduced earlier, a **Dialogic OD mindset** upholds the perspective that transformational change is socially constructed through language, communication, and shared meaning-making that results in a narrative shift. The change practitioner uses a variety of OD methodologies with a focus on this mindset to engage with emergent issues or questions through participatory inquiry, thus sparking generativity and transformational change. The change practitioner may then support self-organized communities to take action on achieving their goals, to stay focused on their purpose, and to amplify new and emerging narratives. This requires masterful Dialogic OD consulting.

Masterful Dialogic OD consulting is inclusive of the ideas of Schein's seminal works on process and humble consulting and of Merron's work on masterful consulting (Merron, 2006; Schein, 1999, 2013, 2016). Process consulting is aligned with Dialogic OD because of Schein's articulation of the consultant as a helper instead of an expert who makes a "diagnosis" of the client's situation (Bushe & Marshak, 2015b; Marshak, 2020). In Schein's most recent work, the process consultant relies on humble inquiry in the moment, which is characteristic of a dialogic approach and working in complexity, and which helps the client figure out their next move (Schein, 2013, 2016). However, Schein himself notes in the foreword of the Dialogic OD text that in practice, he operated in the grey zone because: "I would have labeled what I did as moving with agility between Diagnostic (expert or doctor) and Dialogic (process consultant) OD…" (Schein 2015, p. x).

In using the term "masterful consulting," I mean, like Merron, that "mastery is not a destination, nor is it a thing one does. Instead it is a journey of a lifetime that knows no ending point" (Merron, 2006, p. 182). The alignment of a masterful consulting orientation to Dialogic OD is clear also in the following:

> Masterful consultants know that the magic is not in the models, but rather in the intangibles: the learning process, the consultant's relationship to the client, and the consultant's character. Masterful consultants behave more congruently with their beliefs because they examine their own behaviour deeply and fully. They are also deeply committed to the client having freedom of choice, ownership of the process, and valid information upon which to make decisions. (Merron, 2006, p. 377)

These two models together integrate consulting with a Dialogic OD mindset. The change practitioner using masterful Dialogic OD consulting is attentive to their strategic positioning, to the psychodynamics of the client-consulting relationship, to the principles of their practice, and to their conduct or simple rules from a complexity perspective. The table below outlines these elements of masterful Dialogic OD consulting in practice.

Table 2-2: Components of Masterful Dialogic OD Consulting

Strategic positioning (From Merron, 2006)	Psychodynamics of the client-consulting relationship (Merron, 2006 & Schein, 1999, 2016)	Principles of practice (Selected from Schein, 1999, 2016)	Simple rules of conduct (From Merron, 2006 & my practice—see case-in-point below)
Establish a Co-creative * Empowering Partnership: 1. Develop a client-centered partnership. 2. Share knowledge openly and freely. 3. See the quality of your inner stance as a catalyst for transformation and learning.	The consultant is seen as having knowledge power (of the field, group dynamics etc.), not just process expertise. However, that power is used clearly, responsibly and in alignment with the co-creative empowering partnership. The consultant recognizes the client has positional as well as tacit organizational power to bring to the transformation and ownership of the process (Merron, 2006). The consultant acknowledges that in a society that privileges expertise and competition, the client may initially feel in a "one-down" position and may be reactive as follows: 1. Resentment and Defensiveness (*I know what I'm doing!*) 2. Relief (*Thank God you are here to help me!*) 3. Dependence and subordination (*Tell me what to do.*) 4. Transference (*you are just like the last consultant I encountered.*) The consultant does not fuse with these reactions but works to create status-equilibration and shift the client to the co-creative empowering relationship (Schein, 1999, 2016). *I have some power and you have some power—how do we combine them to co-create a way forward of your choosing?*	1. Today's problems are too complex to rely only on diagnosis. 2. Focus on building consulting relationships based on commitment, curiosity and caring. 3. Everything you do is an intervention. 4. Always stay in touch with the current reality. 5. It is the client who owns the problem and the solution. 6. Go with the flow of the conversation. 7. Timing is crucial. 8. Everything is a source of data; errors are inevitable—learn from them. 9. When in doubt share the problem. 10. Help the client clarify their next adaptive action or move.	1. Always tell the truth. 2. Commit to learning. 3. Bring your whole self. 4. Play a big game. 5. Listen deeply. 6. Ask powerful questions. 7. Co-create action.

*Co-creative is my addition to Merron's empowering partnership because knowledge and experience are co-created from a social constructivist worldview upon which Dialogic OD is based.

I have added "co-creative relationship" to the empowering partnership model that Merron proposes. I align with the framework of an empowering partnership over the Schein framing of a helping relationship. The helping relationship, although positioned within the shift from an expert mindset, still implies to me what Merron (2006) calls a saviour strategy. I believe instead that the empowering partnership is mutual and that the Dialogic OD mindset is co-creative. Schein does acknowledge this in *Humble Consulting* (2016) in the frame of joint exploration and collaboration required in the relationship, but it is still within the context of the humble consultant as a helper.

Finally, practitioners in the Grey Zone of Change must practice the principles of **self-as-instrument of change** (Seashore et al, 2004). Not only is everything happening externally and in the interactions between the practitioner and client/sponsors' data, but so also is the practitioner's moment-to-moment experience. Change practitioners understand that their reactions and interventions directly affect change outcomes and that they are part of and instrumental to the change process. They also understand that the unit of transformation they have the most control over in the Grey Zone of Change is the self. Fundamentally, the change practitioner's ability to hold a non-anxious presence and manage their own and the client's anxiety is essential to Masterful Dialogic OD consulting. Anxiety is contagious and creates a field of angst and fear that can immobilize all who get caught in it. This can make it difficult to move into productive reasoning and action. A non-anxious presence, on the other hand, can neutralize a negative energy field and move people back into forward-moving action (Marshak, 2016).

Practitioners in the Grey Zone of Change must commit to understanding their intuitions and reactivity. They must move them from the unconscious realm to the conscious realm. Once aware of their own experience, they can make informed choices about actions and interventions that serve the co-creative empowering partnership with the client and/or the group they are working with. If there is a singular diagnostic skill that a change practitioner in the Grey Zone of Change must have, it is the capacity to diagnose their own experience and respond to each dialogic interaction in a self-differentiated way. This means that they are connected enough to the current reality of the client's experience to understand it, while separating themselves from any reactivity they may have in the moment, so that they can continue to be effective and masterful. Self-differentiation means that the practitioner uses their experience as data, parks their reactive response when they feel "hooked" by something in the client system, and makes an appropriate intervention instead (Bushe, 2010; Seashore et al., 2004). As some of my senior colleagues have said of this phenomenon, our choice in the midst of reactive situations is to:

- *Get curious, not furious.*
- *Respond not react. We ought to be first responders, not first reactors.*
- *You need to have IT (the experience), not let the IT have you!*

The table below provides an example of how this may work.

Table 2-3: Self-as-Instrument: Example of Managing Practitioner Reactivity

1. Dialogic Interaction	2. Practitioner's Unconscious reactions	3. Conscious Sense-making	4. Co-creative Empowering Response
Client, sounding angry *"That group will never come along. They don't get it!"*	Emotions: • Matching client's anger • Shame signal of feeling flushed Wants to: • Agree with the client • Defend self Instead, goes to 3.	Thoughts: *I'm feeling angry because I am frustrated with that group too!* *Does he think I'm not effective because I've been working with them for a month and nothing is changing?*	Acknowledges situation and own assessment: *I understand it's taking time. I have some frustration too and I'm committed to moving us forward.* Asks: *What possibilities do you see for them to come along?*

This ability to manage one's own reactivity arises from a lifelong journey of learning, maturation, and practice. It requires the discipline that comes from committing to the journey of Masterful Dialogic OD consulting.

Case-In-Point (Navigating Advice from the Field)

So, where does this leave us in navigating the Grey Zone of Change? In a session on Living, Leading, and Facilitating in the Grey Zone of Change at Concordia University, leaders and practitioners worked with the three fundamental principles for navigating the grey zone:

Listening Deeply

Asking Powerful Questions

Co-Creating Actions

I believe that if these three things are all that we do, after acknowledging and understanding the importance of surrendering control and adopting a Dialogic OD mindset, we will become adept at navigating the Grey Zone of Change. This is what is called "minimum critical specifications"—those minimum, "must dos," required to achieve a shared purpose in complex circumstances.

The Concordia group practiced some powerful questions to address sticky issues, wicked problems, and transformational changes in the Grey Zone of Change. They were powerful questions because they evoked transformation. We did not know the answers to them and they signaled the dilemmas and unknowns faced by the collective, thus having the power to support transition, learning & synthesis, and developmental capacity in the Grey Zone. I offer these as food for thought. Test them by applying them to your grey zone experiences:

- ☐ *What is the most inspirational change you see for the future?*
- ☐ *How do you want to serve that future?*
- ☐ *What is the purpose?*
- ☐ *If we have a sense of where we need to go, what keeps us from going there?*
- ☐ *What would change if we played more in the Grey Zone of Change?*
- ☐ *What is needed at this moment to bring us together to connect without ego?*
- ☐ *What are the beacons that will guide and hold us through the grey zone? How will we find them?*
- ☐ *What do we want?*
- ☐ *What is my/our role?*

I invite you to try these on, working them through with others in the grey zone with you and watch for what emerges. I will say more about these minimum specifications in Section 3.

Core Questions & Guidelines: Navigating the Grey Zone of Change

I offer 10 questions for further inquiry in navigating the Grey Zone of Change as individuals, as leaders, and as change practitioners. In exploring each of them, I invite you to explore specific examples, observable behaviours, and/or data on which you are basing your responses.

1. What response strategy is my Grey Zone of Change situated in?
   - A) Reactive (crisis management/fire-fighting)
   - B) Status Quo (resisting change by maintaining an attitude of "This is the way it's always been.")
   - C) Proactive (anticipating and designing the emerging future)
2. What mindset shifts do I need to make?
3. How am I using my agency in the Grey Zone of Change?
4. How am I taking care of myself in the Grey Zone of Change?
5. What am I doing to foster conditions for generativity in the Grey Zone of Change?
6. Where am I using the logic of attraction?
7. Where am I using the logic of replacement?
8. How will engaging from a Dialogic OD mindset serve me?
9. What do I need to develop to practice masterful Dialogic OD consulting?
10. How am I holding myself accountable to managing my reactivity (self-as-instrument) in the Grey Zone of Change?

Some guidelines to consider that will help you navigate your Grey Zone of Change include:

1. If you are in a leadership role, consider partnering with a change practitioner to help you determine your next adaptive actions or to move through your grey zone situation. Do this as frequently as needed as the situation evolves.
2. Get clear about what Dialogic OD mindset, masterful Dialogic OD consulting and self-as-instrument skills you need to develop. Create your development plan based on that. You may conduct a narrative feedback process where you interview your stakeholders to inquire into what skills you might further develop. The focus of the narrative feedback is learning, not diagnosis. You ask stakeholders from an appreciative perspective for stories or examples where you were at your best in navigating a grey zone situation. You then probe for what strengths they witnessed and what they would have wanted more of. You use that feedback to determine your learning and development opportunities.
3. Create your self-care plan. Answer:
   a. How will I manage my energy in the grey zone?
   b. How will I build in space for the things that renew me in the grey zone?
   c. Who are my support people and networks for self-care in the grey zone?
4. Create plans for developing the core minimum requirements for effectively navigating the grey zone. In day-to-day interactions, you can practice the following:

    a.   Listening deeply. Practice listening fully to others without interrupting.

    b.   Asking Powerful Questions. Practice asking a question you are curious about after you have listened to others, without first sharing your own opinion in response.

    c.   Co-Creating Actions. Focus on empowering others to choose their next adaptive action or move.

5.   Practice managing your own reactivity by doing the following in day-to-day interactions. When you are triggered or notice that you are acting reactively:

    a.   Pay attention to interactions that you are triggered by or tend to be reactive in.

    b.   Observe what others are saying or doing that is evoking the reactivity in you.

    c.   Anticipate or observe the impact of your reactive response.

    d.   Make a conscious choice to respond in ways that build a co-creative, empowering relationship.

Summary

Navigating the grey zone requires conscious attention, mindset shifts, and a high level of skill and capability. Fundamentally, individuals in the Grey Zone of Change require a learner's mentality and a willingness to hold self and others accountable to making the required shifts. The leader's challenge in navigating the Grey Zone of Change is fostering the conditions to define the way forward. The leader is not the architect and owner of the change effort, but a partner in it. This requires practicing transformational leadership and fostering the conditions for emergence and generativity. The change practitioner's role is perhaps the most involved role in the grey zone as it nests the experience of individuals and leaders. In addition to a Dialogic OD mindset, successful change practitioners in the grey zone practice masterful Dialogic OD consulting and the principles of self-as-instrument-of-change. In successfully navigating the Grey Zone of Change, if only three actions were practiced, they would be Listening deeply, Asking Powerful Questions, and Co-Creating Actions.

In this section, I have proposed the qualities and mindsets required to navigate the Grey Zone of Change. In the next section, I turn to presenting a comprehensive framework for facilitating transformations in the Grey Zone of Change.

Application

Journal on your own or, in the spirit of social construction, find a trusted partner, triad, or group who are in a grey zone situation with you to discuss and provide you with feedback. Partners in this conversation should provide specific examples and observations to anchor their feedback. Journal your insights, using them as a basis for determining one action you can take.

1. What is your experience of navigating the Grey Zone of Change as an individual? How do others experience you? What ideas from the Navigating section were most impactful for you?

2. What is your experience of navigating the Grey Zone of Change as a leader? How do others experience you? What ideas from the Navigating section most resonated with you?

3. What is your experience of navigating the Grey Zone of Change as a practitioner? How do others experience you? What ideas from the Navigating section most energized you?

SECTION 3

Facilitating in the Grey Zone of Change

In this section, we will explore the following key questions.

- What is a framework for facilitating transformation in the Grey Zone of Change?
- What is required in Initiating the Transformation?
- What is required in Facilitating the Journey?
- What is required in Sustaining the Transformations?

Framework Overview

I offer a structured framework for supporting transformations in the Grey Zone of Change for precisely the issues raised in Section 1 about the dynamics of the grey zone. Having a framework or a structured method to share with leaders provides some certainty and structure, which is one way to reduce anxiety on the road to transformation. The absence of a frame amplifies the confusion and anxiety inherent in the grey zone. We know that a group or team without clear purpose and boundaries will flounder, while those with a clear framework will flourish. The same applies to the Grey Zone of Change. From a systems lens, a framework provides a clear container. If the container is too tight, it is too restrictive with no room for generativity and productive engagement. However, if it is too loose, it will amplify confusion and anxiety.

Therefore, a framework creates a container within which the necessary interactions can occur. That allows coherent emergence to arise instead of the dysfunction of incoherence that can occur in groups with weak or nonexistent boundaries. We see how this is being addressed through the numerous structured Dialogic Organization Development (OD) methodologies that have emerged. For example, the Dialogic OD volume (2015c) lists 40 methods; others are noted on the Dialogic OD website (https://b-m-institute.com/links-to-materials-on-the-practice-of-dialogic-od/). The second edition of *The Change Handbook* detailed 61 methods and the most recent cataloging of collaborative change practices for the next edition yielded a library of seven volumes and over 100 methods (Nexus4Change, n.d.). A similar field of practice, *Liberating Structures,* does a good job of conveying the role and need for structure in order to unleash the participation and generative capacity of participants in change processes (Lipmanowicz & McCandless, 2014). Note also that this is similar to the phenomenon of "matching the system" or, as the consulting community would say, "meeting the client where they are at." This is the dynamic through which a leader or intervener is deemed credible when they demonstrate in style and/or process, being both part of the system as well as being different from it. For example, it is easier to transform an authoritarian culture into a participatory one by at first mandating participatory processes until they become "the way things are" (Axelrod, 2011, pp. 156-157).

Any single framework is only a framework. If it offers a useful container for guiding others through transformational change, then it is valuable. A metaphor that may be useful for thinking about the role of Dialogic OD frameworks is a man-made body of water that might spread at will, but structures such as a dyke/dam/river course may be used to guide it into a desired shape or direction. Even the oceans have simple rules—ebbs and flows and tides—that guide how and where they arrive and stop at the shore. Please hold this framework in that spirit.

A Comprehensive Framework: Facilitating Transformation in the Grey Zone of Change

A comprehensive framework for facilitating transformation in the grey zone is presented below. Previously, I introduced three stages of the Dialogic OD Process: Initiating the Inquiry, Facilitating the Journey, and Sustaining Transformations (Gilpin-Jackson, 2015). Since then, I have systematically worked through these stages in my consulting practice with clients and have used them to teach Dialogic OD practice to graduate students. I have now integrated feedback from these experiences by adding the consulting outcomes at each stage and the group tasks required to go through the sub-zones of the grey zone. I have also included leader and practitioner roles at each stage.

Essentially, transformation in the Grey Zone of Change requires that everyone in the system is committed to and ready for change. Leaders must practice transformational leadership and foster conditions for generativity and either assume the role of a change practitioner with the mindset and skills to navigate the grey zone, or partner with one. I call this the trifecta for success in the Grey Zone of Change; it assumes the involvement of a change practitioner or a leader who holds the mindset and skills required.

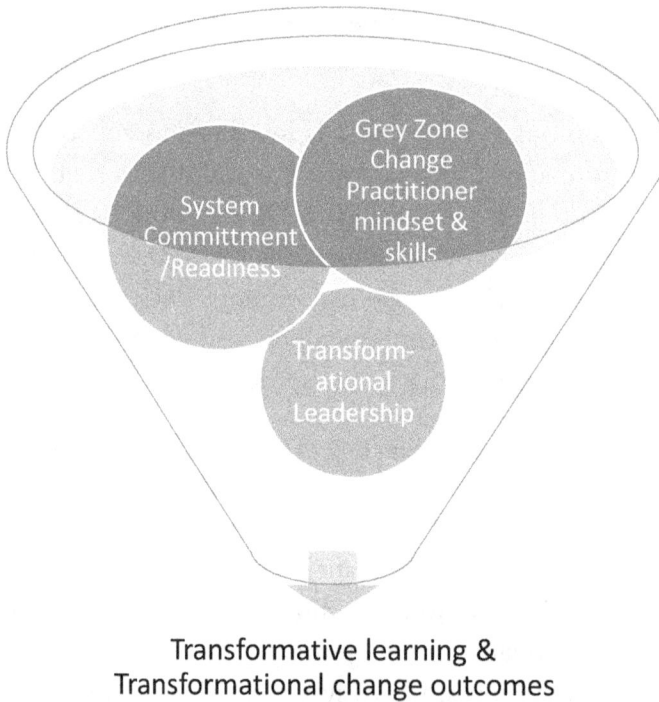

Transformative learning &
Transformational change outcomes

Figure 3-1: Conditions for Transformation in Grey Zone Change

Initiating the Inquiry

At this stage, the change practitioner makes first contact with the client system, knowing that the initial contact is an intervention. ***The practitioner is assessing the client for readiness, preparing the client and themselves for the transformation, and ensuring that there is a clear contract.*** An overarching goal is to establish a co-creative empowering partnership, which places the client at the center. The practitioner establishes being supportive of the client's learning and transformation, in service of co-creating the next adaptive actions to their complex challenges.

In assessing for readiness, the change practitioner asks questions to understand the client's situation. The inquiry can cover a range of questions that are open and evocative and can be informative (overview of current state), affirmative (surfacing what is already working), critical (surfacing systems dynamics, assumptions and possible disruptions), generative (surfacing creative ideas), and strategic (surfacing future vision, plans and actions) (Southern, 2015). When initiating the inquiry, the focus ought to be on questions that foster transformative learning to uncover the dilemmas, feelings, and critical assumptions of the client. There must be an intentional focus, not just on "the situation out there," but also on the client's direct experience.

1. What dilemmas/issues/tensions are you experiencing?
   a. What is the current state you would like to transform?
   b. What are your judgments about this situation?
2. How do you feel about the change?
   a. What are your hopes and fears?
3. What assumptions do you and others hold about this situation?

The practitioner listens deeply to the language of what is being said (including metaphor and story use) and what is not being said, and probes more deeply as they sense where the client may be open to change or where the client may need to be challenged (Marshak, 2020). This is integral to preparing the client for transformation and is an opportunity for the change practitioner to model the type of practice into which the client and their organization will be invited. Although it is helpful to have in mind the questions to ask, it is more important to be present, to attend to the flow of the conversation, and to ask appropriate questions as they arise naturally. It is from deep listening and questioning that transformative learning occurs and generativity emerges.

Table 3-1: Comprehensive Framework for Facilitating Transformation in Grey Zone Change

Dialogic OD Mindset & Self-As-Instrument			
Stages of Transformation	Initiating the Inquiry	Facilitating the Journey	Sustaining Transformation
Transformative Learning Process: Mezirow's 10 phases of transformation (Mezirow, 2009)	1. Identify a disorientating dilemma. 2. Examine feelings of fear, anger, guilt, or shame. 3. Engage in a critical assessment of assumptions.	4. Recognize that one's discontent and the processes of transformation are shared. 5. Explore options for new roles, relationships and actions. 6. Plan a course of action.	7. Acquire knowledge and skills for implementing one's plans. 8. Try on new roles. 9. Build competence and self-confidence in new roles and relationships. 10. Recalibrate one's life on the basis of conditions dictated by one's new perspective.
Grey zone— sub-zones	Help people transition.	Help people transition and learn.	Help people transition, learn and develop as a whole.
	Focus on possibility and courage.		

Practitioner Roles/ Consulting Outcomes	1. Assess client system & practitioner's own readiness. 2. Prepare for transformation by supporting the group and leader in their tasks at this stage. 3. Establish the co-creative empowering relationship with the client. 4. Contract with the client.	5. Shepherd "the container." 6. Co-create intentional design. 7. Facilitate as needed.	8. Support evaluation. 9. Support sustaining structures.
Group Tasks	1. Engage with the emergent ideas. 2. Work on their own transition. 3. Share experiences.	4. Generate images/metaphors /narratives for current state and the emerging future. 5. Design the transformation process.	6. Embed developmental shifts. 7. Articulate new narrative and system boundaries.
Leader Tasks	Model Transformational & Generative Leadership Practices		
	1. Define purpose of transformation. 2. Define boundaries (negotiables and non-negotiables). 3. Share personal story. 4. Craft powerful invitation.	5. Remove obstacles. 6. Support experimentation and innovation. 7. Model generative leadership.	8. Evaluate outcomes. 9. Implement top actions. 10. Support, spread and scale.

⟵⟶ Masterful Dialogic OD Consulting & Shared Practices ⟵⟶

The intent of this early initiating phase, as per Averbuch (2015), is to filter responses through this lens:

- Is the situation ready/suitable?
- Are the people in the client system ready?
- Am I (the practitioner) ready?
- What are my choices if I assess that the client and situation are not ready for transformation?

We will proceed for the moment with the assumption that the client and system are ready to work toward the transformations they are asking for. We discuss choices to consider when the situation does not appear right for transformation in the next section.

I have found it helpful to use a matrix to map readiness against complexity as a guide to assessing whether clients are ready for the transformations they are requesting. The proposal is that situations with moderate to high readiness and high complexity are best suited for dialogic or blended methodology practice with a Dialogic OD mindset. That means that both dialogic and diagnostic methodologies can and should be used as needed in the situation. For example, traditional surveys, live polling, or pulse data on people's experience is still useful in my practice, especially when working in a large system where everyone cannot be brought together at the same time. Information collected can then be integrated into dialogic process designs as one data point rather than "the truth." In dialogic processes, further "data" may be generated live from peoples' shared experiences. Every interaction, as it occurs, is data for the change journey.

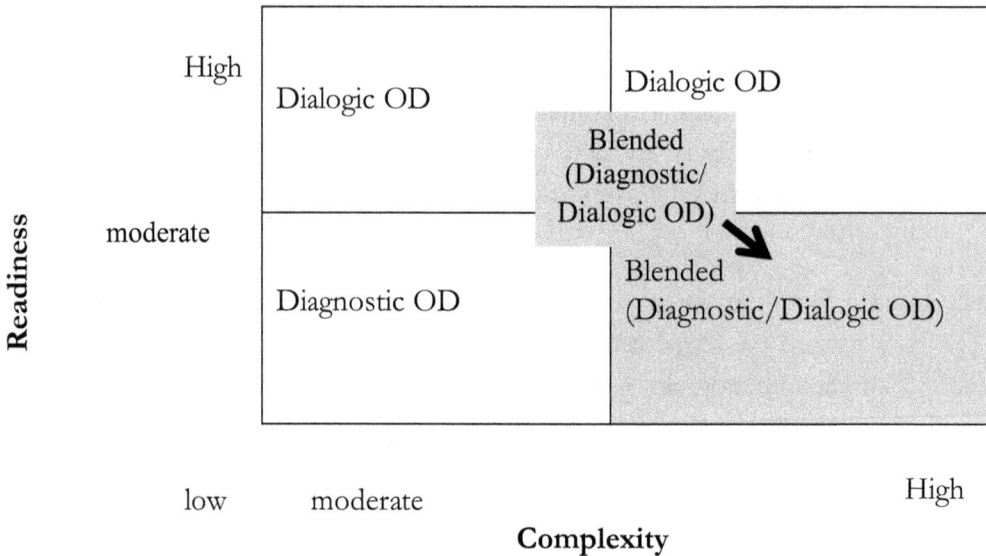

Figure 3-2: The Grey Zone of Change Diagnostic Grid for Blended Diagnostic/Dialogic OD Practice. First printed in Organization Development Practitioner 45(1)

In addition, note that, at this initiating stage, every level of "client" is engaged with in this same way, with iterative spirals of assessment done with the sponsor, the operational lead(s), and the actual group(s) or representative of the group(s) who are impacted by the change (Averbuch, 2015).

The initiating phase must end with a clear contract that outlines:

1. Co-created purpose/goals and intentions of the transformation journey.
2. Deliverables with as much clarity as possible regarding the purpose of the transformation, what and how preparation and planning will be completed (e.g. with a design team), and what methodologies will be used.
3. Roles and expectations of all involved.

The change practitioner must try to include as much information as possible, knowing that clarity will help reduce client anxiety. At the same time, they must leave explicit room for the unknown and the unknowables, bearing in mind that psychodynamics of the Grey Zone of Change will emerge and will need to be addressed.

Note that the client's introduction to the group(s) concerned may happen in the initiating phase or in the facilitating-the-journey phase. Meeting the group(s) can sometimes be a bridge between the initiating and facilitating stages of the process. It is critical at this point that people are invited in a way that enrolls them in the purpose and possibilities ahead. The framework I use for invitation is from Peter Block (2018), which incorporates the following:

- Name the possibility they are being invited to convene around.
- Specify what is required of everyone should they choose to attend.
- Make the invitation as personal as possible.
- Be clear that a refusal carries no cost.

Once the process starts, the group can begin to share stories that connect them to the purpose of the transformation, to work through what they may lose as they embark on the transition, and to reflect on what they will gain.

The Practitioner's Transformation Journey in the Initiating Stage

As noted in Section 2, the practitioner is not exempt from the transformative learning journey and is, in fact, actively engaged in it throughout. As Bill O'Brien has said: "The success of an intervention depends on the interior condition of the intervener" (Presencing Institute, 2017).

Take for example, the current world system. In so many conversations, the people around me—family, friends and practitioners in Leadership, Organization Development and Social Change are asking—*What can we do in the current socio-political climate facing North America and the world?* This is a complex question, with no easy answers. The ensuing dialogue and responses have ranged from fear and hopelessness ("The system is about to bifurcate!") to apathy ("Let's wait and see."), to desperate activism ("I'll march if it's the only thing I can do!"), to thoughtful analysis and committed action ("Here's what I see, here's what I can do today."). None of these responses are right or wrong. I have found myself at all points on the continuum, depending on the day or on the latest breaking news. These responses are all normal human reactions to complexity, to the unknown, and to the chaos of the grey zone. A disorienting dilemma ushers in a disturbance to a world that is ready for change. We are able to choose how we engage the disturbance. What does this mean for me when I am asked to facilitate or host dialogues related to some of the most pressing social change issues of our time around immigrant relations, women's participation in governance, or global black African identities?

For me, I feel a disorientating dilemma as a knot in my stomach that typically sits there, unflinching, until I pay attention. The knot is my signal that I have something to listen to, learn about, or understand better. At this stage, all that is required is the recognition that I am perturbed and my willingness to engage, rather than avoid the sources and conversations about my disorientation. However, as I initiate inquiry, I must be willing to examine my own emotional state regarding the situation and to identify the automatic and usually reactive emotions associated with disorienting dilemmas. This can involve feelings of fear, anger, guilt, or shame. I believe this is the hardest phase of transformative learning. People either get stuck or they chose to undergo the process of learning and change. It is difficult, because where there are adverse consequences and human impacts, engaging our emotions means simultaneously facing our own part, and/or processing the factual reality, and/or realizing the impacts.

This means making choices about how to engage further. This is the place at which I can choose to be in denial and bury my head in the sand, or to confront the raw, painful emotions arising from our current socio-political environment.

If for example, I, a black, African, woman, who has been a refugee and an immigrant and is a Christian with a Muslim family, cannot be honest about my emotional responses to the current world context, how can I facilitate others to see all sides of the situation and learn from it? I cannot help others through this process if I cannot face and immediately process and address emotional responses that may be painful for me as I facilitate. I must be able to hold hurt and project faith, love, hope, and trust for others, so that I can hear their pain too. And there are times where I must also be radically authentic about what hurts. I do this by sharing in equally radical love, such that trust and safety are maintained for further dialogue. I have had many moments as a consultant or facilitative leader in the past three years to engage with my client systems in this way. This isn't easy. But to get to transformation, I, and we, must engage our emotional responses, no matter how painful they are. As we say in the facilitation world, there can be no shared agreement without first achieving shared understanding. This is the goal in initiating the journey.

The ability to acknowledge and effectively process emotions leads to the stage of a conscious, critical examination of assumptions I have held before the disorienting dilemma. For example, an assumption I have heard from many in the refugee and immigrant community and that I have faced myself is: *"This cannot be happening HERE!"* The assumption that North America has a flawless democracy, where corruption and a dictatorship-style leadership are impossible, has been broken. This and its related assumptions ("It's safe HERE but not THERE where I left as a refugee!") are now in question and require critical examination. What does the reality that detrimental occurrences ARE happening HERE mean for me and those like me? For others? What will the intended and unintended consequences be for America, Canada, Mexico, and those s-hole countries? What will the generational impact be for families who have been separated in the complexities of illegal immigration and the dreamers? We must continue to critically face the implications—for unless we do, we cannot effectively and constructively engage in transformational change. We must seek more just outcomes in our organizations and in the world than those we are facing today.

Facilitating the Transformation Journey

At this stage, the practitioner, having established a co-creative empowering partnership with the client and group(s) (see Section 2), can now focus on intentional design in preparation for the transformation journey, whether it is in the form of an ongoing immersive consulting or strategic change engagement(s) or an event(s).

The goal at this stage is to ensure that interventions are "fit for function." Of the hundreds of methodologies out there, change practitioners must select the ones that are appropriate to support the actual goals of the client. Methodologies can be OD's first-generation (diagnostic), second-generation (action learning, which is focused on reflection and learning in real-time to determine actions), or third-generation (dialogic) methodologies. Designing for transformation also involves ensuring that the needs of the entire system are met at all levels, not just one level. Recall from Section 1 the proposition that successful large-scale interventions *are a function of contextual conditions (C), personal transformation (tP) and organizational transformation (tO), where contextual conditions have a multiplier effect on the attainment of transformation.* TE = C [tP + tO]. Intentional design for transformation will entail addressing:

- Context: Choose methodologies that create the right conditions for the core group task at hand – e.g., shared decision-making processes, strategy and visioning (vision conferences), work redesign (scenario planning, customer experience walkthroughs), and so on. In addition, it is clear from the study from which this emerged that contextual factors were impacted by how well the facilitation design created safety and community—that is, a strong and appropriate container from a systems perspective. Significant here is the invitation process to ensure all participants are well enrolled, and a design that reinforces the physical and psychological space throughout as a "safe" and welcoming container (Corrigan, 2015). This is also the place to ask: What systems, structures, and processes must be addressed to ensure the long-term sustainability of transformations?
- Personal Transformation: Build into the Dialogic OD interventions opportunities for personal transformation such as coaching, real-time observation and feedback, leadership dojos (working with the leader's self as source of power), and other developmental interventions.
- Organization Transformation: Build in methodologies that support the group to co-create and develop new ways of working together. Beyond methodology, I integrate here elements of design and practices that allow the group to process collective experience and make meaning together. This includes debriefs or after-action reviews, fishbowls, story circles, ancient wisdom cafés, survey feedback sessions, narrative development/storytelling, conversation cafés, world cafés, etc.

Designs are ideally co-created with the input of those who will be engaged in the process. The idea is that the change practitioner will work with a design team to define purpose and desired outcomes of the facilitation journey as well as the experience they want to create. Logistics of the engagements are also defined. The practitioner then guides the design process, bringing forward proposals for the design team to work through to ensure structures are in place to move toward the purpose of the change. The practitioner's role throughout the preparation, and every dialogic (inter)action that ensues, is to protect "the container" that has been co-created throughout the "initiating the inquiry" stage. To this end, the practitioner must exercise the principle of masterful Dialogic OD consulting by "telling the truth" when people in the system may be taking actions that adversely affect the dialogic container.

The beauty of the dialogic mindset is that when sessions are well-designed, the learning needed to achieve transformation is automatically embedded. Participants leave having had shared experiences, having co-created options, and having decided on next actions together. They build relationships and make connections in ways that are meant to be part of the transformation process.

In all of this, the leader participates fully, not as a bystander, but by taking on the role of removing obstacles and testing the ideas being generated. The group's task is to explore all options and experiment with the possibilities. As they do so, the anxieties of the Grey Zone of Change lessen, and are replaced with the positive group energy that comes with increased engagement and influence. The differentiation and coherence of a system further along the grey zone continuum begins to emerge. As I describe in the next section, by the end of the "facilitating the journey" stage, a new narrative should have begun to emerge, even though the process may not be linear or without obstacles. This is essentially the surfacing of the new system after assumptions of existing narratives that may be limiting for the emerging future have been examined and shed or changed. This narrative shift is the essence of transformation and the outcome of a Dialogic OD mindset and practice in the grey zone.

One important note is that outputs of the process must be well-documented in ways that can be easily and visually shared. Visual facilitation and collaborative document-sharing platforms are two ways in which this can happen. This makes it possible to continue sharing the outcomes broadly, engaging those stakeholders who may have missed in-person sessions and continually widening the circle of involvement as needed. The process of continued involvement of the whole system between "events" has been called a walkthrough and is meant to be more than a "report back" or presentation; rather, it is a meaningful and tangible sharing of the experience (Axelrod & Axelrod, 2006; Axelrod, 2011).

The Practitioner's Transformation Journey in the Facilitating Stage
Evidence from the transformative learning community (Daloz, 2000) shows that certain actions support people through these phases of the transformation process. These apply equally to practitioners:

Find a Transformative Learning Community: Recognizing the shared nature of discontent is the first phase of the actual "facilitation" phase of transformation. To practice what we preach, practitioners must find at least a partner and ideally a community of practitioners to support them through the transformation journey to examine their own untested assumptions, doubts, fears, and hopes. Through reflective discourse and exploration, practitioners move toward self-transformation as their worldviews are stretched and expanded by listening to the diverse experiences of others and by being able to freely share their own. It is in its simplest form, the experience of knowing that *I am not alone in this learning journey and I have a safe space in which to go through my own process* that unlocks transformation.

In the last couple of years, as the connection between OD theories and social change and justice issues have come back into focus, I have found myself in too many dialogues and sessions on power, privilege and social justice. As I live in the Pacific Northwest, work in senior leadership and in a profession where I can count on one hand the number of black women and men colleagues I have encountered, there has been ample opportunity for me to become the container and throughway for current social justice and diversity issues. This has been an emotional and exhausting journey as I have also been on the receiving end of unconscious biases and experiences of the very social dynamics and concerns being examined. My buffer has been my triad of OD practitioner friends. We are three women who identify as global Africans and who use our OD practitioner skillsets in a variety of diverse contexts, on and off the continent (Gilpin-Jackson, Owusu, & Okonkwo, 2017; Okonkwo & Owusu, 2016). We have met monthly or bi-monthly via Skype for four years. We have processed our dilemmas, disorientations, and growth edges together, becoming a transformative learning community for each other. This has been my island of sanity in these times, providing a nexus of hope that gives me the strength to go back out into the world and to keep on working for transformation.

Explore New and Different Options: As the transformative learning journey continues, new and different questions and options begin to emerge. Change practitioners working in the grey zone will often find themselves asking the same questions of themselves that they are asking their clients.

- What can I do now? What role do I want in this situation?
- What new relationships will support me in my own self-transformation journey?
- Where and with whom do I feel safe to share my own disorienting dilemmas about the current world system to engage in genuine discourse and learning?
- How do I want to be in relationship with those around me who hold similar and different worldviews?
- What is my own identity and worldview of the various moral questions we face and how does that colour my world?
- What new outcomes do I want for myself?

Commit to Action: Finally, when leading a transformation, there may be many opportunities for practitioners to take small actions to model support for the process, another sense in which being part of the client system, but also apart from it, makes a big difference. To facilitate transformation, we must go first and commit to taking actions toward our own self-transformation, which may inspire others to take action also. For example, in my internal executive leadership roles, I am often coaching and facilitating leaders through large-scale transformation. In a recent coaching situation, the leader I was working with was expressing being stuck "because it always seems to be the same issues!" I reminded the leader that the issues may be similar to past ones, but the people and networks involved are different. I shared what actions I had taken and what I was committed to doing with my own team in the same circumstance and asked: "What possible actions might you take?" My client lit up and said: "Thank you for reminding me!" and started generating ideas.

Sustaining Transformations

Intention must translate into action before transformative learning can be fully realized, integrated and sustained. Oftentimes transformation journeys fall apart in the space between planning and action.

The change practitioner at this stage must support the evaluation of the work and coach the system through designing and implementing sustaining structures to uphold the transformation, both organizationally and individually. It is at this stage that all aspects of transformation throughout the process are solidified. What is done or not done at this stage impacts whether the organization will realize the new narrative that has emerged and experience the coherence of a system that has successfully gone through the Grey Zone of Change. In many ways, this may be the most important stage of an entire intervention in the Grey Zone of Change.

Organizationally, this requires amplifying the change through deeper exploration of the viable ideas and experiments from the facilitation phase, nurturing the best ideas, and embedding the infrastructures required for ongoing success. Some experimentation may have started during the facilitation phase, but deeper prototyping and feasibility testing of innovative ideas for the purposes of embedding change happens here (Roehrig et al., 2015).

This is the stage at which the client actively takes steps to integrate and embed the transformative learning gained by acquiring knowledge and skills for implementing plans, exploring different roles and actions through trial and error, building confidence and competence in relation to what the new system requires, and encouraging people to integrate transformed worldviews. This is all easier said than done because transformation—a fundamental change in worldview and behaviours as a result of expanded perspectives—is hard work. Transformed thinking requires consistent action for the change to be evident in people, in relationships, and in organizations. This, of course, is true of any behavioral change—it requires practice to become habit.

There are many theories about what gets in the way and stops us from making behavioural changes, including the ideas of immunity to change because of underlying competing commitments, which I often work with to support leaders who may be getting stuck at this stage (Kegan & Lahey, 2001). However, in my experience, when deep change has occurred, the ensuing behavioural changes come much easier. I believe that sustaining transformations requires patience and perseverance in addition to the passion that transformation at first evokes. Groups at this stage must work equally hard to embed their developmental shifts, to articulate their new narratives and boundaries, and to create the sustaining structures required to bring the new system into coherence.

For example, I co-led the launch of a Centre of Excellence in Health Care Leadership over the past seven years. The concept has taken three major forms (the Collaboratory, the Leadership Academy ,and now the Centre), through which the concept was loosely explored and tested. In 2017-2018, the idea of a Centre of Excellence started to emerge and coalesce, sparking generative ideas of what might be possible in a series of group and one-on-one sessions to enroll and widen the circle of partners in the conversation. One leader offered the metaphor and corresponding narrative of the Centre as a lighthouse within the organization that beckons to leaders and guides their directions, which resonated. In spring, 2019, the Centre officially launched with a series of events and a trend survey that addressed leaders, practitioners, and scholars in the field. However, it quickly became apparent that stronger sustaining structures were needed. To fulfill that need, my co-leads and I worked with the network of stakeholders to co-create an internal steering committee, an external advisory committee, a design team, and a larger working group that have all self-organized to take on various tasks. This has allowed the work to begin to grow and scale and to become embedded into the scaffolding of the organization. This new way of working and coherence would not have been possible without persistent work over the preceding 18 months to co-design the sustaining structures, especially after previous "failed" attempts.

The Practitioner's Transformation Journey in the Sustaining Stage
So, what happens when you, as a change practitioner, also try a new role or action as part of a transformation and it doesn't work? Say for example, as a facilitator, your experience of the world has you explore questions about your own assumptions regarding current polarized issues and conflicts. As a result of realizing a transformation, you decide to take on facilitating diversity dialogues and hosting social change discussion circles. In your first attempts, you feel incompetent in your new role. You say things that participants take issue with. One person gives you feedback about how an innocuous comment you made caused offense. You have no choice but to keep learning and facilitating to build your confidence and competence, which will only happen if you are willing to persevere through the discomfort of seeming failures. How do you persevere? You simply do. There is no formula. I conducted a series of

research interviews with some of the most extraordinary transformational leaders I have ever met; every one of these leaders had mustered the will, determination, and grit to persevere in the dreams that their transformation experiences had evoked for them. Each in their own way expressed that when they are deeply connected to their dreams and the underlying source of their transformation experiences, they are unstoppable—no matter what obstacles come their way (Gilpin-Jackson, 2014).

We must keep facilitating the complex dialogues that are surfacing in our organizations and in our world until we become as skilled and masterful as possible at hosting them. I believe that in the current state of the world, it is better to try, fail, learn, and try again than not to try at all. Inaction is colluding. Trying, failing, and learning is leading, and it is the call of the grey zone of our times.

The Shared Practices

I introduced the minimum specifications for navigating the grey zone in Section 2 and note them here as foundational to the comprehensive framework for facilitating transformation in the Grey Zone of Change. I call them shared practices because everyone in the grey zone needs to practice them for progress to be made. To reiterate, the practices are:

Listening Deeply

Asking Powerful Questions

Co-Creating Actions

These minimum specifications for success in the Grey Zone of Change require that everyone involved adopt a specific dialogic way of being. This way of being, synonymous with the Dialogic OD philosophy of co-construction, is what I call transformational listening and questioning that allows for emergence and generativity. Chené Swart has written about these simple practices that make the biggest difference in Dialogic OD from a narrative perspective (Chené Swart, 2013, 2015). Robert Marshak's work on Deep Listening and Transforming Talk is also essential reading for how to engage as such in the consulting relationship (Marshak 2004, 2020). I have adopted and have used the following recommendations from their work and from my own experience with narrative inquiry.

Transformational Listening:

1. Be willing to be transformed in the conversation.
2. Be passionately interested in how people describe their experiences.

3. Notice and resist automatic tendencies to interrupt, judge, think about solutions, or fuse with the storyteller. Notice these tendencies and practice letting others complete before chiming in.
4. Think of and explore the implications of the narrative in the past, present, future.
5. Listen for and use the vocabulary of the conversation (the language, text, ideas, images, narratives) to explore places where you are intrigued.
6. Ask when you are not sure you understand.

Transformational Questioning. Ask open questions that:

1. are transparent, providing context based on the reason, purpose and direction of the conversation.
2. you do not know the answers to.
3. emerge from the discussion (not your pre-defined questions).
4. detach each person from the "problem" in question.
5. explore the assumptions, issues, and experiences that people raise.
6. unlock the imagination and possibilities arising from the conversation.

Listening and questioning set the context for emergence and co-creation. However, co-creating actions requires using both skills as well as being willing to move beyond some of the dissonance and disagreements that can arise when seeking alignment to action. To co-create, I use the simple rules of inquiry that build adaptive capacity in complexity and in the Grey Zone of Change. I add the five rules of adaptive action, also from complexity thinking and Human Systems Dynamics (Human Systems Dynamics Institute, 2020d, 2020e):

1. Turn judgment into curiosity.
2. Turn disagreement into shared exploration.
3. Turn defensiveness into self-reflection.
4. Turn assumptions into questions.
5. Turn fixed solutions into adaptive action (ask "What?" "So what?" and "Now what?").

Case-in-Point

Here is an example of how I have applied this framework.

I was approached by a client in the education sector. As the new head administrator of a school system, the leader was interested in a strategic planning process to refresh the organizational context. The idea was to (re)confirm vision, mission, and working principles that would guide strategies going forward. I met with the client to initiate the inquiry and, in listening to the language used in the stories and responses to my questions, I assessed the client and situation as ready for the transformation journey.

The grey zone was that this was a very stable environment where, on the surface, everything was going well. However, the client had several layers of dissonance between what was espoused and what was happening in practice. It appeared that people were very comfortable with "the way things are" and also had different perspectives of what that was. From a systems dynamics perspective, the agents in the system were misaligned; system coherence was based on maintaining the status quo by avoiding the deeper patterns and issues that threatened disruption. The client was not satisfied with the status quo and wanted clearer alignment to their purpose. They wanted adaptive action to address key adaptive challenges that were surfacing.

The client wanted a personal shift from "an education administrator to an education leader." The hope was that all leaders would make this shift once it started to be modelled from the top. The client wished to move from spending time in tactical and technical detail to spending time in strategic conversations. The vision was a shift to spending more time mentoring than problem-solving and, in the future, supporting leaders in regularly learning and having meaningful conversations, perhaps even hosting a leadership book club. The client was clear about a desire to involve and engage everyone in a new way of being and also knew that the refreshed vision, mission, and direction of the organization had to originate from all stakeholders. These stakeholders all had different philosophies of what needed to happen in the organization; they were not interacting or engaging with each other. The leader was committed to shifting that and to attaining a new level of coherence with a shared understanding of their goals. In a brainstorm of what this process might be called, the client decided on "Community Conversations: Learning from our Past, Designing our Future." We moved forward to contracting with clear co-created purpose and a draft of process deliverables through a proposed Dialogic OD journey that would impact every level required for transformation.

As we transitioned to the next stage, we drafted a process for designing the future, which was revised and finalized with various stakeholders in previously scheduled group meetings with the leader. The final design entailed the following:

1. Leadership coaching
2. Blended diagnostic and dialogic methodologies:
   a. Survey to all stakeholders, internally and externally, about the vision, mission and values alignment of the organization
   b. Community Conversations that all stakeholders could sign up for. The identical session was offered at different times to ensure that all had the opportunity to participate. The design entailed "world café" rounds in which small groups discussed various questions or issues that were identified from the survey, surfaced insights, and harvested implications for moving forward.
3. A staff session followed the community conversations for further collective sensemaking of the outcomes of the sessions. They focused on distilling all

feedback into a six-word story and tagline for the institution, thus co-creating a new narrative, using the shared practices of listening, questioning, and collaboration. This was shared broadly for any final feedback before it was adopted.

This process achieved the desired collaborative objectives, not simply because of the process itself, but because I believe the leader modelled and held to the core principles of a Dialogic OD mindset in the Grey Zone of Change. I witnessed a leader as committed to self-development as to the change process. A leader willing to both set clear boundaries and to give up control to allow for generativity on the part of stakeholders involved in the process. A leader willing to try a new and unclear way for the sake of forging a greater future than was already being realized. The leader was so committed that I was able to step aside as a facilitator. My role shifted to supporting via coaching and feedback on the dialogic interactions that occurred throughout the sessions facilitated by the leader. and to functioning as a design partner. The final proposals were largely accepted by the Board.

At the end of the community conversations, one external stakeholder whom I happened to know in another context, wrote a text expressing that: "This is the first time [this institution] has ever done anything like this in the 12 years that I've been here. I like the new direction they are taking…"

I continued to coach this client and had a front-row seat to their commitment to progress toward their personal and organizational goals and to seeing the actions that were proposed and implemented taking effect. They continued to use blended methodologies in a system that had low dialogic readiness but moderate to high complexity because of the number of agents involved and the historical context. For example, they used 360-degree feedback for senior leaders while working toward fostering leadership dialogues in new ways (e.g. leadership tip/book club conversations). However, the overarching ethos within which the client and I engaged was a Dialogic OD mindset.

Core Questions & Guidelines: Facilitating transformation in the Grey Zone of Change

I offer 10 questions for facilitating transformation in the Grey Zone of Change as leaders and as change practitioners for you to consider and to start working through.

1. What are the core challenges with facilitating transformation in the Grey Zone of Change?
2. How do I know if the client situation is ready? Who needs to be ready in the system?
3. What are the most important inquiry questions I must ask to prepare the various client(s) for transformation?
4. What personal transformations must I be ready to contend with in this grey zone situation?
5. What design will be most fit for function in this situation?
6. Where will I find my most suitable transformative learning community to support me through this grey zone experience?
7. What is needed to ensure the container remains safe throughout the process?
8. What is required to nurture changes in myself and in the system?
9. What is required to embed the changes into the structures of the organization?
10. What skill(s) must I develop to model a Dialogic OD mindset throughout this grey zone?

Guidelines for facilitating transformation in the Grey Zone of Change:

1. Review the comprehensive framework for facilitating transformation in the grey zone and consider your strengths and opportunities.
2. Use a past or current case to walk through each stage of the transformation process to identify possibilities for further action.
3. Consider engaging with other individuals, change practitioners, and/or leaders with whom you can walk through your case to generate further insights and to clarify your next steps.
4. Use the framework to guide you through your next grey zone transformation.

Summary

Facilitating transformation in the Grey Zone of Change requires strong commitment at all levels of the system, transformational leadership, and masterful Dialogic OD consulting. These three conditions together form a strong container within which leaders and practitioners can work effectively to support groups to succeed with their transformational change goals.

With these three conditions in place, each agent has a role to play. The practitioner assesses the situation, prepares the client and themselves for transformation, and co-creates a contract that provides enough clarity to reduce client anxiety but is still realistic about emergence. The group does its generative work that comes with working through the sub-zones of the Grey Zone of Change—transition, learning & synthesis, and group development—and engages in the transformation processes designed. The leader practices transformational leadership and fosters generativity by giving up control of the change design while working to implement and make way for the experimentation, evaluation, and amplification of the changes.

Throughout this process, the minimum shared practices by all involved are listening deeply, asking powerful questions, and co-creating actions. When everything aligns, the results are simply magical. This was the case in the original grey zone case study I published (Gilpin-Jackson, 2015). Although I note some positive feedback and outcomes, one particular memory is seared in my mind that I did not include in the publication of that case. The magical moment happened in a visioning session. We had come through some initial difficult group dynamics. The leadership team had reapplied for their own roles and there had been some movement within them. We had started the Dialogic OD process as defined, initially with low trust among the group as we completed leadership assessments and started to have transition conversations. The team finally began to show developmental shifts as my co-facilitator and I named the patterns we were seeing and the shifts they needed to make to transition themselves and their teams. When we arrived at the day-long visioning session, I was braced for a process that would be long and arduous and that would take all the masterful Dialogic OD consulting we had to pull off a unified vision for the group.

We went into the day as designed, leading the group through classic visioning exercises and debriefs that ended with data on the wall about the common themes of everyone's vision. We then sent them into groups to synthesize and craft vision statements. I remember feeling tense as the groups worked, reviewing over and over what our consensus-building and final decision-making process would be if we did not arrive at a vision. We had accounted for every level of collaborative decision-making. We had even accounted for moving to a crowd-sourced democratic process through which the larger organization would give input on the draft statements. and finally the leader would make the decision if there were still pieces to be resolved. None of it was necessary. When the groups came back and shared their visions, all four were nearly identical, save a word or two. It was the moment at which a new coherence emerged in that system. The five-word draft vision statement they ended up aligning with became their new unifying generative narrative. Not only that, but it was broadly accepted when the leader took it on a road show across the organization with other framings of the new system.

I have witnessed this high level of coherence as many times since then. I have also witnessed more modest levels of success and sometimes a system bifurcation when the core conditions do not come together and alignment and coherence does not emerge. So, what lessons have I learned from living, leading, and facilitating in the Grey Zone of Change? I offer some of my experiences and thoughts in the next section.

Application

Journal on your own or find a trusted partner or triad to discuss the following. Determine one action that your insights inspire.

1. What has been your best Grey Zone of Change experience?

2. What has been your most challenging Grey Zone of Change experience?

3. What lessons are you taking forward from both Grey Zone of Change experiences?

4. Practice Transformational Listening & Questioning in a group setting. Sit knee-to-knee and each:
   - Share a story that most illustrates the lessons you are taking from your grey zone experiences.
   - After each person shares, the others ask transformational questions that emerged from listening. Decide how many to ask each other depending on the time you have.
   - After all have shared and asked questions, each can share one new insight gained.

SECTION 4

Lessons from the Grey Zone of Change

In this section, I explore:
1. What are some lessons from the Grey Zone of Change?
2. What gets in the way of success in the Grey Zone of Change?
3. What about when people are not coming along/ready/willing?
4. What are some lessons from narrative and storytelling (and humanizing practices)?
5. How can I support myself and others in the Grey Zone of Change?
6. Why lean into the discomfort of this unconventional practice to be successful?

I start with the caveat that I offer this section only as one perspective and as a way of sharing my experiences in the Grey Zone of Change. They are not offered as prescriptive or as firm representations of objective truth, but simply as the reflections of my lived experience in leading and facilitating in the Grey Zone of Change. I know that by the time this is published, I will have had more conversations, I will have encountered other perspectives. and I will likely have broadened my horizons about possibilities in the Grey Zone of Change.

Reflections from the Grey Zone of Change

Some overarching reflections I have surfaced at this point in my journey of experiences in the Grey Zone of Change are:

1. We are in a transitional space where new systems are emerging.
2. Effective change and transformation are less about diagnostic or dialogic methodologies and more about mindsets and orientation.
3. Diagnostic and traditional structures are not dead.
4. Dialogic mindsets and skillsets are required.
5. Practitioner, leadership, and system readiness matters.
6. Continuous inquiry through listening, questioning, and co-creating action are needed.

I hope I have made the case for each of these throughout, so I will provide only a brief summary here.

The Dialogic Organization Development (OD) mindset is essential to navigating the grey zone, regardless of the type of OD methodologies being used. It is the mindset that favours the philosophy of social construction, through which conversations and human experience are synonymous with change. We change in interaction with others because we create our reality through the new narratives that emerge from the generativity of our conversations. When we truly connect with each other, we form the narratives we live by. As a participant at a recent conference put it, "Words are things!" Conversations have creative power and that power is amplified when you have a group of people working together to accomplish a shared goal. With this mindset, diagnostic data is just as useful for shared meaning-making as is subjective experience.

Both are data, as is the data inherent in the interactions happening in the moment. Therefore, it is a fallacy to hold Dialogic OD as an ideal to be achieved to the exclusion of traditional diagnostic methods and structures. As was shown, intervening into such traditional structures requires some level of matching the structures or speaking the "language" of the system so that you can be understood.

The grey zone, the space between systems, is filled with unknowns. The best way forward in this space is by listening, questioning, and taking co-creative adaptive actions to experiment and to learn in the unknown territory. None of this is possible without the readiness of leaders, practitioners, and groups to adopt the Dialogic OD mindset. As a result, even as I share these reflections, I continue to hold the inquiry question:

- ***How do we accelerate building the transformational change capacities and practices required of us all in Grey Zone Change and in transitional spaces?***

What gets in the way of success in the Grey Zone of Change?

I wish to continue the conversation started in Section 1 about system dynamics, psychodynamics, and group dynamics to comment on some ways in which related issues may get in the way of success in the grey zone.

System Inertia & Entropy

Remember the basic physics law of inertia? I mean Newton's First Law of Motion that an object will remain at rest or will move at a constant speed in a straight line unless it is acted upon by an unbalanced force. This widely accepted principle reflects only one side of systems life as we know it today based on the complexity sciences, which tell us about the tendency for systems to be every-changing, self-organizing and in motion. When a system remains at rest, it moves towards entropy, whereby the energy within it for productive work gradually dissipates and leads to breakdown, much like what happens with our muscles and bodies without movement. On the other hand, disruptions and signals for change will occur, causing a system to change and to reorganize itself. The same applies to human systems. They are constantly changing, whether we accept that or not. Human systems that ignore signals for change will break down or bifurcate between parts of the system that align with the emergence and parts that do not. Systems that absorb signals generatively will evolve and grow (Eoyang, 2018; Quinn, 2004).

The issue that gets in the way of success in the Grey Zone of Change is when the people within a system, in whole or in part, choose their comfort zone over the unknown of change, which then leads to inertia. Quinn (2004) notes this as choosing slow death over the work of deep change. I am referring here to the <u>continued choice</u> to remain in a status quo state, even after all the work and all the strategies for navigating the grey zone have been exhausted. This is the point at which adults, who are free to choose, decide not to engage the emergence and possibility of the grey zone. This is the scenario in which no amount of coercion or force (the burning platform!) or attractors to change (transformational leadership) has any impact. In theory, the right balance of energy (not so much that it bifurcates and not so little that there's no motivation) should move any system to change. However, in human systems, we must account for free will and for the freedom to choose.

In some cases, individuals' fears and anxieties may lead to a competing commitment to their comfort zone which supersedes their desire for change (see next). It's also possible that system readiness is just not present. When that is the case, the system will either remain stagnant and/or decline, or the parts of the system that want to change will bifurcate either individually or collectively. In other cases, the work already done will be absorbed into the status quo, but will serve as seeds planted for when other conditions of readiness line up to create the tipping point required for change.

Immunity to Change
Sometimes a client may commit to changes or actions but may consistently fall short and even act in opposing ways to doing what is required to make change a reality. This may be due to the idea of competing commitments, as defined by Robert Kegan and Lisa Lahey (2001). They note that when people develop "immunity to changes" they espouse to want, it is because of an unconscious application of productive energy towards equally important competing commitments. Think of this as a fixed mindset, kept in place by unconscious assumptions that remain untested and unexamined. To achieve transformation, we must fundamentally shift fixed mindsets, not just acquire new information. We must shift the very form/structure from which we engage ourselves, our clients, and our world (Kegan, 2000). Kegan and Lahey have offered a diagnostic set of questions for uncovering the competing commitment and underlying assumptions supporting it. I use a client example to illustrate how it works.

1. What would you like to see changed, so that you could be more effective or so that work would be more satisfying?
   - *My client was a founder who was feeling overwhelmed by doing all things in the business and decided to take on significant business expansion. The client committed to bringing in other leaders, to mentor and coach them to take over operations, and to transition to a supportive and business development role.*
2. What commitments does your complaint imply?
   - *The client reported being burnt out, no longer able to keep up with the demands of the business.*
3. What are *you* doing, or not doing, that is keeping your commitment from being more fully realized?

- *What was actually happening was that the client was micro-managing the new team members hired, being directive about what and how they performed the roles they were hired for. The client was still spending 50% plus of their time in the office on operations rather than mentoring and coaching, or engaging in business development. The result was rapid turnover of new hires and a continually frazzled client.*

4. If you imagine doing the opposite of the undermining behavior, do you detect in yourself any discomfort, worry, or vague fear?
   - *The client reported fear of failure if the new team didn't get it right.*
5. By engaging in this undermining behavior, what worrisome outcome are you committed to preventing?
   - *The client was committed to preventing the expansion from failing.*
6. What is your underlying big assumption? [if the opposite of your worrisome outcome occurred]
   - *The client assumed that if the expansion was successful, they would lose status as the business owner and expert and become irrelevant.*

Shifting this required that the client observe and document the impact of their behaviours on themselves and on the new team members. We co-created small test assignments of "letting go" and observing the relevant roles the client was still called upon to fulfil. We designed ways for the client to grow as a learner and collaborator and to step out of the expert role. The client did make slow progress but the initial competing commitment definitely got in the way of the transformation taking hold.

Hysteresis

Another system characteristic that may influence success in the grey zone is hysteresis. It is the systems idea that learning and change are non-linear and that "every phase shift—cognitive, cultural, social, physical—goes through a confusing state where past and future exist side by side…hysteresis explains that the state of a system depends on its history. The past overshadows the present as a change process goes forward" (Eoyang, 2017, p 1). Hysteresis explains the phenomenon where complex adaptive systems seemingly backslide or forget lessons learned until there is enough forward movement for the new to eclipse the old and become embedded. Hysteresis can get in the way of success in the grey zone when humans forget this system tendency and give up before transformation has taken hold. It is why I advocate for patience and perseverance when the conditions seem right but the transformation appears to be taking too long. Given the right conditions, it is literally a matter of time (and reinforcement) before transformational change happens.

Impatience Plus Anxiety

Anxiety is already an issue in the Grey Zone of Change. It is amplified by impatience. Thus, anxiety plus impatience becomes an impediment to successful transformation when different stakeholders respond to system pressures or to their own need for certainty by asking for quick answers. Those who may still be outcome and diagnosis-minded without depth of understanding of what is needed for transformational change may keep asking "Are we there yet?" The drive for quick wins from business sponsors, requests from Boards, and demands from investors can all create performance pressure, which amplifies anxiety. This may lead to a default back to the usual way of doing things that will create short-term success but no long-term transformational change. The leader and/or change practitioner's challenge is to balance delivering short-term wins to stakeholders while continuing to set conditions for transformation.

Triggered clients, triggered change practitioners
As covered in Section 2 and 3, the transformative learning capacity of change agents to self-manage their triggers and reactivity is essential to successful change outcomes. A change practitioner who does not exercise self-as-instrument and self-management with respect to reactivity may amplify already anxious and easily triggered clients. If an unhealthy pattern of interaction ensues between these key change agents who are leaders and holders of the change process, it can get in the way of successful outcomes in any number of ways. System agents may lose faith in the process, the leaders, and the change practitioner. The change practitioner may "fire the client" or be excused from the contract. The leader may decide it is too hard to work toward transformational change and may revert to traditional ways of working.

Other Considerations

What about when people are not coming along/ready/willing?
I am addressing this question because I have been asked it by students, practitioners and leaders alike in a variety of forums. It often comes, understandably, with the exasperation of change agents who have done all they know how to do and are not seeing the expected changes that ought to result. As already covered, that may be for any number of dynamical issues in systems, as well as psychodynamics or group dynamics issues. System agents may have chosen the status quo as per the discussion on immunity to change above. The bottom line for me is that I am always at choice to stay and to keep trying to move transformation forward. I can also choose to leave the system, providing another signal that change is required, one way or another. I, like every other agent in the system, have free will. As a change practitioner, I also believe that I have responsibility to the client system to reassess and/or provide feedback to it that may help influence emerging patterns, whether I choose to stay or not. Either way, a masterful Dialogic OD consultant knows when their work is done. Here are some options.

1. (Re)assess to determine whether the situation is no longer suited for transformation.
   a. Check-in with the client about your observations, remembering that you are in a co-creative, empowering relationship and the client ultimately owns the process and the decisions about how to progress.
   b. If you both agree that there is no will to proceed or to continue with a transformational process, the change practitioner can arrange to transition out of the system and to recommend other resources or consultants with skillsets that may be better suited to the context.
   c. If you both agree there is will to proceed, you will likely learn what was in the way of progress, develop new ways of working, and (re)contract to ensure a successful way forward.
   d. If the pattern continues, (re)assess again as to whether it is a matter of hysteresis, the need for adaptive action, or time to exit the system.
2. Create a container for providing feedback and dialogue about the patterns at play and engage agents in reassessing what may be needed now. In the world of co-construction, a safe container for dialogue about what is happening below the iceberg may well be what is needed to shift a system and be the difference that makes a difference.

On narratives, storytelling (and other humanizing practices)
I am adding a note about the significant role of narrative reauthoring in transformation and development or even as an intervention to create shifts where systems appear to be stuck. Narrative practices are fundamental to a Dialogic OD mindset and practice and have been an integral part of my work. When I was a doctoral student, I became a convert to the power of social constructivism and dialogic ways of being. This was a surprise to me, much like Brené Brown describes in her renowned Ted talk on the power of vulnerability. To me, data was data. It was objective truth and research meant seeking underlying cause and effect relationships through empirical methods. That was, until I met the professor who challenged me not to discount my own subjectivity in research and not to disregard the power of my lived experiences. I was introduced to interpretivism and the use of subjective self and experience as research, and to social construction as a way of creating knowledge together.

All of a sudden, huge puzzle pieces of understanding myself opened up. It was a transformative experience. I came to the realization that I could use as data my own lived experiences as a black woman of African descent who was born in Germany but who grew up back on the continent and then immigrated back to the West as a refugee. Suddenly, I had language and context to "analyze" while better understanding my lived experiences on the margins and as an outlier of all the communities into which I didn't quite fit. I could make that understanding transparent and I could theorize from experience in ways that made it possible for others to build models for testing my hypotheses. My insider-outsider experiences were valid. It was a humanizing experience. I continue to collaborate on quantitative research studies and to understand their role in research and generalizable knowledge-creation. However, my Dialogic OD mindset and experience-based ways of knowing and learning are predominant for me. I came to narrative inquiry in the process and started using it both in my research and practice (Atkinson, 2007; Clandinin & Connelly, 2000; Riessman, 2008). By the time I discovered Chené Swart's work and met her in person, I was already practicing as a consultant and facilitator in very similar ways to those outlined in her work on reauthoring from a narrative therapy perspective (Swart, 2013). I have continued to learn and practice from this narrative orientation, further validated with the work in Dialogic OD and transformation, showing the importance of narrative to change process and practice.

Stories matter in the Grey Zone of Change because they move the teller and the listeners from their heads to their hearts and create a different field of knowing and learning together. They allow for extra-rational, expressive and intuitive ways of knowing to become part of the decision-making and co-construction process, which is a core way of accessing transformation (Yorks & Kasl, 2006). In short, our stories matter, and they get woven together to form the narratives by which we live, individually and in organizations (van den Nieuwenhof, 2013).

In my experience, when leaders and groups appear to be stuck in the grey zone, (re)introducing narrative and other humanizing ways for people to connect with each other and to their shared purpose shifts the dynamic back to a generative one. The beauty of stories is that they can also be used to scale. We all have a story, and the stories of individuals, small groups, and entire systems can be linked to create a generative future together. It is why leadership communication and collective narrative formation such as Ganz's model of "self, us, now" – of using a story process to find a collective WHY are effective (Ganz, 2007; Sinek, Mead, & Docker, 2017).

For example, I often ask participants in sessions in which I have used Dialogic OD and narrative methods to share the impact of the experience at the end of the session. Here is one example of their responses.

Figure 4-1-Experience of a Grey Zone Change session

How can I support myself and others through the Grey Zone of Change?

I briefly touched on the need for self-care in the Grey Zone of Change in Section 2. There can be physical as well as mental impacts on everyone working through the Grey Zone of Change, especially because it is transformational work. Yes, there will be lots of positive affect and creative energy as generativity kicks in, but the work of transformative learning can also be psychologically draining. Have you ever attended a one-day conference that was meaningful for you and highly engaging and left feeling ravenous and exhausted? That's what I mean. So how can you take care of yourself in the Grey Zone of Change? It really comes down to the basics when you are in the midst of the work, especially the group engagements.

1. Be well-rested.
2. Stay well-fed and hydrated.
3. Pace yourself. Build in time and space for reflection and processing.
4. Maintain boundaries. Be clearly committed to both your yesses and your nos.
5. Hold to your values and leadership practices.
6. Engage with trusted others and your support community to help you recharge and get unstuck as needed.

Supporting others is inclusive of the above. Here are some possibilities.

1. Offer to coach and mentor others.
2. Engage in a learning community or community of practice.
3. Take initiative to host further dialogues when there is a perspective you are seeking to understand.
4. Ask for and offer help.
5. Respect others' needs.

Why lean into the discomfort of unconventional practice to be successful?

So, if working through the Grey Zone of Change comes with these edges and the discomfort of learning and development, why choose it over traditional ways of working? For me, this calls for a more intuitive response. My immediate response to the question is: "Why not?" Or as one of my siblings loves to ask: "What is the alternative?" The outcome of staying the same and undergoing change in the way it has always been done in a simpler world is inertia, status quo, and slow death. The alternative is to walk wide-eyed and anxious into the grey zone, knowing that the possibility of transformation lies at the other side. I have offered suggestions throughout this book, but a more direct way to discovering whether something matters enough to you to embark on this journey is through the spirit of profound inquiry put forth by Peter Block (Block, 2003). Block reminds us that for anything that truly matters, the answer to how is yes; we can then examine our relationship to the choices we are making.

Table 4-1: Peter Block's Questions from: The Answer to How is Yes: Acting on What Matters. 2003. San Francisco, CA: Berrett-Koehler Publishers.

HOW?	YES!
How do you do it?	What refusal have I been postponing?
How long will it take?	What commitment am I willing to make?
How much does it cost?	What is the price I am willing to pay?
How do you get those people to change?	What is my contribution to the problem I am concerned with?
How do we measure it?	What is the crossroad at which I find myself at this point in my life/work?
How are other people doing it successfully?	What do we want to create together?

Case-in-point

I will use two similar cases to illustrate some of these lessons from the Grey Zone of

Change. I was invited to work with a struggling non-profit group working with a marginalized population. Two board members of the organization had seen me facilitate a narrative process and thought it might help them through their crisis. Their Board and leadership had been at an impasse for a while and the situation seemed to be devolving. When they spoke to me, the two Board members were certain that the organization was on the brink of bifurcation and they themselves were ready to move in another direction. Their experience was that there had been a disagreement that they had not been able to resolve, about how to address a critical make-or-break decision. They were willing to give it one more try, they said. I agreed to work with them and we contracted for two sessions. In the first, I met with the full board and simply sat around the table with them in inquiry. I asked them what questions they needed to answer to move forward to possibility; I asked what their negotiables and non-negotiables were. I asked for their hopes and fears and I asked for the assumptions they had about the situation. They responded tentatively, but steadily shared responses that created a hope that they were at least willing to give it another try, because of their shared commitment to the people they served.

In the second session, we went through a narrative (re)formation process. They engaged with each other around their stories of "self, us, now" and into the future. They spoke to each other about their purpose for doing the work. At that juncture, I sensed the emergence of possibility as they moved into generativity. They were soon co-creating their alternative options around the decision that had seemed impossible. They ended with clear agreements about decision options, implementation plans, and actions to take if old patterns and possible hysteresis emerged. They did not believe that reverting back to how things were was an option. If their work ended, the people they served would be significantly impacted. I learned after following up that the Board and organization had pulled through. They aligned on the decision even under pressure to change their minds. The leaders who had contacted me told me they continued on together and that trust among the group had increased. They believed it was storytelling and engaging in a way they had never done before that had made the shifts possible.

A year or so afterwards, one of the same leaders contacted me to work on a different non-profit Board. This one worked internationally, but the circumstances were similar. They were at a crisis point, stalled at a crucial decision that wasn't being made because of bifurcation on the Board, which took the form of classic group dysfunctions of pairing, fight or flight, and co-dependency. Some signs of group trauma were even evident in the hyperreactivity and stuck behaviours of some of the members. I knew the issues were significant when, shortly after engaging in inquiry with the leader, nearly every pairing or individual holding power that had been described, made their case to me in emails that were pages long. A few members sent equally long replies in response to my simple acknowledgment email. I expressed concern to the leader who had approached me, but agreed to engage with the group as a collective for another inquiry and then determine whether or not to continue.

At the beginning of that inquiry session, the dynamics were similar to those in the first case. We seemed to be progressing tentatively but steadily. I observed openness to different perspectives through the questions they were asking each other. They appeared to be moving toward generativity by brainstorming and co-creating their options. However, within the last hour of the day, right when it looked like needed decisions could be explored, everything began to unravel. My observation is that two members who were locked in a power struggle triggered each other. In spite of my best interventions, they landed in positional places and refused to move. I experienced the pattern I had been warned about. I was feeling hooked in the situation because I hate to fail but was recognizing that we were missing the core of a Dialogic OD mindset. The two in question were not open to learning; the rest of the group was stuck in patterns of aligning with one or the other so that no real listening, questioning or co-creating was occurring; and I was struggling to manage my reactivity and impatience. When I shared my observations about the patterns, there was silence, followed only by a final request to me from the group to complete another round of working with them.

My experience of the second round of work was of hysteresis—some movement forward, followed by big leaps back whenever someone in the group was triggered. I got them to the point of acknowledging the pattern, but they continued to choose the status quo and never arrived at a generative new image of themselves. I exited the engagement leaving them with clear thoughts, observations, and inquiry which I emailed to all of them. When I followed up a few months later, the Board member who had originally contacted me was in the process of resigning, as were three others. The system was bifurcating and changing of its own accord. Those who had aligned with the status quo were remaining, and those who were committed to deep change for themselves and for the groups they were serving were choosing deep change.

Core Questions & Guidelines: Lessons from the Grey Zone of Change

Here are 10 questions to consider overall regarding lessons in the Grey Zone of Change.

1. What are my choices when I (re)assess a client's readiness and find they may no longer be ready for transformational change?
2. How do I manage my experience of impatience if a client is slow to change or is in hysteresis (a seeming regression from change progress)?
3. What might I do to reframe the pressure for performance and quick wins in the Grey Zone of Change?
4. What else can I do to expand a client or group's vision of possibility when they appear to be moving away from the Dialogic OD mindset/approach to transformation?
5. How do I hold the tension of understanding others' free will when working with groups or causes that matter to me?

6. How do I like to be supported when I am in the Grey Zone of Change?
7. What support can I offer others in the Grey Zone of Change?
8. What (re)humanizing practices might enhance my practice in the Grey Zone of Change?
9. How might I use narrative methods to support emergence and transformation?
10. What is required of me?

Some guidelines for working with these lessons in the Grey Zone include:

1. Amplify narratives and narrative elements (e.g. metaphors, symbols, imagery etc.) that point to the emerging future or that offer generativity in the grey zone. Remember that narrative elements form a culture.

2. Review your grey zone situations for signs of inertia, entropy, and hysteresis. Host conversations with the client and groups involved and explore questions like the following to determine what amplifies the changes underway and rejuvenates the transformation.
   a. What stories signify that there is progress? Ensure they share and harvest the conditions from the stories that are supporting progress.
   b. How might we create more of the conditions supporting our progress?
   c. What is needed to keep the transformation progressing?
   d. What feels stuck? Explore this if the group dynamics require that what is stuck be directly named and addressed, Otherwise, work on amplifying progress as per a to c above.
   e. Test commitments to the transformation – use the Yes questions from Peter Block's: *The Answer to How is Yes:* in Table 4-1 to facilitate conversation in small or large groups and determine as a collective the commitment of the group. This dialogue in itself will create change by shifting awareness within the group of where they are individually and collectively. This will create the context for where the group needs to go next.

3. Engage anxious clients in a timely manner with the purpose of triggering learning and co-creating action to manage the anxiety.
   a. What is your current experience of the grey zone?
   b. How are you feeling about the situation?
   c. What do you need more of and less of?
   d. What worry is underlying the anxiety experience?
   e. What assumptions do your worries imply?
   f. What do you have control of in the situation?
   g. What do you need to let go of?
   h. What are you learning about yourself and your leadership style in the Grey Zone of Change?
   i. What next adaptive move is emerging?

Summary

This journey through my present understanding of the Grey Zone of Change has been reflective and illuminating. Making sense of my thinking and deriving meaning from my grey zone experiences have reinforced the core lessons about the power of the dialogic mindset regardless of methodology. They have reminded me of how much leader, practitioner and system readiness matter to transformation. Transformation can never be forced but it can be influenced in the direction of possibility, emergence and a new coherence, primarily by choosing to step out of comfort and into deep change. Sometimes, internal and external pressures and the choices of others lead to a system bifurcation or a collective abandonment of transformation processes. Change practitioners need to be aware of this and they need to be willing to choose whether or not to engage further. All of us have a choice to examine our own ideologies and defenses when we are questioning "how," rather than choosing "yes." I believe that, when it matters, those who are ready will always find the doorway to yes and to new possibilities.

Courage Required: It all Matters

A final word, In the course of engaging with this work, I have added another sub-zone to the Grey Zone of Change experience—the zone of possibility and courage. (See Figure 4-2.) As described throughout Section 2, the courage to say yes and to keep going is essential to transformation. The appreciative lens that sees possibility, even when system pressures seem insurmountable, can make the difference between forward motion and inertia.

Every dialogic interaction meant to create transformation in the grey zone matters. In the case in which my non-profit client group bifurcated, do I consider that a failure? My reactive self wants to say, "Yes, it was a failure." However, when I pause to breathe and to engage in conscious thinking, I remember the analogy of seed-planting and the complex adaptive system concept of the butterfly effect (Human Systems Dynamics Institute, 2003f). Oftentimes, the impact of our small actions is impossible to see or to know in real time because complex adaptive systems are impossible to control or to predict. Our actions today are like seeds that need time to germinate in order to sprout and to grow. Though the client did not achieve their collective transformation goal of finding a way forward to stay together, I have no idea what personal reflection or transformations may have occurred for those who were more open, nor do I know what learning might transfer into a future situation. Just like the butterfly effect, each small action in one part of the system can lead to a landslide shift downstream in another part of the system. As I do the work toward human systems transformation, that is my constant hope. I know that I am here, doing the work I do, because my ancestors fought for my right to do so. The continued transformation of our organizations and world into places for human thriving and flourishing matters too much.

Sub-Zone of Transition
Sub-Zone of Learning & Synthesis
Sub-Zone of Group Development
Sub-Zone of Possibility and Courage

Figure 4-2: Expanded Model of the Grey Zone of Change

How about you?

What courage is required of you as you work for transformation in your Grey Zones of Change?

Application

Personal Reflection:

1. What Grey Zone Change challenges matter most to you right now?

2. Using your list from #1, work through the Peter Block questions in Table 7 to discover your *yes* in areas you find yourself asking *how*.

HOW?	YES!
How do you do it?	What refusal have I been postponing?
How long will it take?	What commitment am I willing to make?
How much does it cost?	What is the price I am willing to pay?
How do you get those people to change?	What is my contribution to the problem I am concerned with?
How do we measure it?	What is the crossroad at which I find myself at this point in my life/work?
How are other people doing it successfully?	What do we want to create together?

3. Journal: What courage is required of you?
    a. What narrative do you want for yourself a year from now?
    b. What first steps might you take to get there?
    c. What support might you need?
    d. Consider reaching out to a trusted partner, colleague or community of learning to share the results of this exercise.

REFERENCES

Aguiar, A. C., & Tonelli, M. J. (2018). Dialogic organization development and subject–object dualism: A social constructionist perspective on dialogic methods in an organizational context. *The Journal of Applied Behavioral Science, 54*(4), 457-476. doi:10.1177/0021886318796491.

Atkinson, R. (2007). The life story interview as a bridge to narrative inquiry. In D. J. Clandinin (Ed.), *Handbook of narrative inquiry: Mapping a methodology* (pp. 224-241). Thousand Oaks, CA: SAGE.

Averbuch, T. (2015). Entering, readiness and contracting for dialogic organization development. In G. R. Bushe & R. J. Marshak (Eds.), *Dialogic Organization Development: The Theory and Practice of Transformational Change*. San Francisco, CA: Berrett-Koehler.

Axelrod, D., & Axelrod, E. (2006). Conference model. In P. Holman, T. Devane, & S. Cady (Eds.), *The Change Handbook: The Definitive Resource on Today's Best Methods for Engaging Whole Systems* (pp. 207-211). San Francisco: CA: Berret-Koehler.

Axelrod, R. (2008). *How to get people to care about what you find important*. Dick Axelrod.

Axelrod, R., Axelrod, E., Beedon, J., & Jacobs, R. W. (2004). *You don't have to do it alone: How to involve others to get things done*. San Francisco, CA: Berrett-Koehler.

Axelrod, R. (2011). *Terms of engagement: New ways of leading and changing organizations* (2nd ed.). San Francisco: Berrett-Koehler Publishers, Inc.

Berkana Institute. (2013). Our theory of change. Retrieved from https://berkana.org/about/our-theory-of-change/.

Bion, W.R. (1961). *Experiences in Groups And Other Papers*. London: Tavistock

Block, P. (2003). *The answer to how is yes: Acting on what matters*. San Francisco, CA: Berrett-Koehler Publishers.

Block, P. (2018). *Community: The structure of belonging* (2nd ed.). San Francisco, CA Berrett-Koehler Publishers Inc.

Bridges, W. (1991). *Managing transitions: Making the most of change*. Philadelphia, PA: De Capo Press Books.

Bushe, G. R. (2010). *Clear leadership: Sustaining real collaboration and partnership at work*. Boston, MA: Davies-Black.

Bushe, G. R. (2019). Generative leadership. *Canadian Journal of Physician Leadership*. Vol 5 (3).

Bushe, G.R. (2020). The dynamics of generative change. *BMI Series in Dialogic OD*. North Vancouver, Canada: BMI Publishing.

Bushe, G. R., & Marshak, R. J. (2015a). Introduction to the dialogic organization development mindset. In G. R. Bushe & R. J. Marshak (Eds.), *Dialogic Organization Development: The Theory and Practice of Transformational Change*. (pp. 11 - 31). Oakland, CA: Berrett-Koehler.

Bushe, G. R., & Marshak, R. J. (2015b). Introduction to the practice of dialogic OD. In G. R. Bushe & R. J. Marshak (Eds.), *Dialogic Organization Development: The Theory and Practice of Transformational Change*. Oakland: CA: Berrett-Koehler.

Bushe, G. R., & Marshak, R. J. (Eds.). (2015c). *Dialogic organization development: The theory and practice of transformational change.* CA: Berrett-Koehler.

Bushe, G.R. & Nagaishi, M. (2018) Imagining the future by standing on the past: OD is not (just) about change. *Organization Development Journal, 35*:3, 23 – 36.

Cameron, K., & McNaughtan, J. (2016). Positive organizational change: What the field of positive organizational scholarship offers to organization development practitioners. In W. Rothwell, J. Stavros, & R. Sullivan (Eds.), *Practicing Organization Development: Leading Transformation and Change* (4th Edition ed.). Hoboken, NJ: John Wiley & Sons.

Clandinin, D. J., & Connelly, F. M. (2000). *Narrative inquiry: Experience and story in qualitative research* (F. M. Connelly, Trans.). San Francisco, CA: Jossey-Bass.

Corrigan, C. (2015). Hosting and holding containers. In G. R. Bushe & R. J. Marshak (Eds.), *Dialogic Organization Development: The Theory and Practice of Transformational Change.* San Francisco, CA: Berrett-Koehler.

Cranton, P., & Taylor, E. W. (2012). Transformative learning theory: Seeking a more unifed theory. In E. W. Taylor & P. Cranton and Associates (Eds.), *Handbook of Transformative Learning: Theory, Research and Practice* (pp. 3-20). San Francisco, CA: John Wiley and Sons.

Daloz, L. A. P. (2000). Transformative learning for the common good. In J. Mezirow (Ed.), *Learning as transformation: Critical perspectives on a theory in progress.* San Francisco, CA: Jossey-Bass.

Dooley, K. (1996). A nominal definition of complex adaptive systems. *The Chaos Network, 8*(1), 2-3.

Egan, T. M. (2002). Organization development: An examination of definitions and dependent variables. *Organization Development Journal, 20*(2), 59 - 70.

Eoyang, G. (2017). *Hysteresis.* Human Systems Dynamics Institute. https://www.hsdinstitute.org/resources/hysteresis.html

Eoyang, G. (2018). *Changing change: Influence what you cannot control.* Human Systems Dynamics Institute. https://www.hsdinstitute.org/resources/changing-change.html

Fortune Magazine. (2019). *Change the world.* Retrieved from https://fortune.com/change-the-world/2019.

Ganz, M. (2007). Worksheet: Telling your public story: self, us, now. Kennedy school of government.

Gilpin-Jackson, Y. (2013). Practicing in the grey area between dialogic and diagnostic organization development. *Organization Development Practitioner, 45*(1), 60-66.

Gilpin-Jackson, Y. (2014). Resonance as transformative learning moment: The key to transformation in sociocultural and posttrauma contexts. *Journal of Transformative Education, 12*(1), 95-119. doi:10.1177/1541344614541547.

Gilpin-Jackson, Y. (2015). Transformative learning during dialogic OD. In G. R. Bushe & R. J. Marshak (Eds.), *Dialogic Organization Development: The Theory and Practice of Transformational Change.* (pp. 245-268). Oakland, CA: Berrett-Koehler Publishers.

Gilpin-Jackson, Y. (2016). Understanding participant experiences in large-scale organization development interventions (LODIs) in a complex healthcare system. *Leadership & Organization Development Journal, 38*(3), 419-432. doi:https://doi.org/10.1108/LODJ-12-2015-0284.

Gilpin-Jackson, Y. (2018). It's time to make Organization Development our client. *Organization Development Practitioner, 50*, 7-15.

Gilpin-Jackson, Y. (In-Press). *Transformation after trauma: The power of resonance*. New York, NY: Peter Lang Publishers.

Gilpin-Jackson, Y., & Crump, M. (2018). Practicing in the grey area between dialogic and diagnostic organization development: Lessons from ***Another*** healthcare case study. *Organization Development Practitioner, 50*(4), 41-47.

Gilpin-Jackson, Y., Owusu, S., & Okonkwo, J. (2017). *We Will Lead Africa: Volume 1* (Vol. 1). South Carolina: Create Space Publishing.

Heifetz, R., Linsky, M., & Grashow, A. (2009). *The practice of adaptive leadership: Tools and tactics for changing your organization and the world*. Boston, MA: Harvard Business Press.

Holman, P. (2010). *Engaging emergence: Turning upheaval into opportunity*. San Francisco: CA: Berrett-Koehler Publishers.

Holman, P. (2015). Complexity, self-organization and emergence. In G. R. Bushe & R. J. Marshak (Eds.), *Dialogic Organization Development: The Theory and Practice of Transformational Change*. San Francisco, CA: Berrett-Koehler.

Holman, P., Devane, T., & Cady, S. (2007). *The change handbook: The definitive resource on today's best methods for engaging whole systems*. San Franscisco, CA: Berrett-Koehler.

Hopper, E. (2003). *Traumatic Experience in the Unconscious Life of Groups*. London: Jessica Kingsley Publishers.

Hopper, E. (Ed.) (2012). *Trauma and Organizations*. London: Karnac Books.

Human Systems Dynamics Institute. (2020a). Nothing is intractable: Find your next wise action. Retrieved from https://www.hsdinstitute.org/

Human Systems Dynamics Institute. (2020b). Complex Adaptive Systems: Retrieved from https://www.hsdinstitute.org/resources/complex-adaptive-system.html

Human Systems Dynamics Institute. (2020c). CDE Model: Retrieved from https://www.hsdinstitute.org/resources/cde-model.html

Human Systems Dynamics Institute. (2020d). Inquiry: Build Adaptive Capacity. Retrieved from https://www.hsdinstitute.org/resources/resources-inquiry.html

Human Systems Dynamics Institute. (2020e). Adaptive Action. Retrieved from https://www.hsdinstitute.org/resources/adaptive-action.html

Human Systems Dynamics Institute. (2020f). Butterfly Effect. Retrieved from https://www.hsdinstitute.org/resources/butterfly-effects-blog.html

Johnson, B. (1992). *Polarity management identifying and managing unsolvable problems / Barry Johnson*. Amherst, Mass: HRD Press.

Kegan, R. (1982). *The evolving self: Problem and process in human development*. Cambridge, MA: Harvard University Press.

Kegan, R. (1994). *In over our heads: The mental demands of modern life*. Cambridge, MA: Harvard University Press.

Kegan, R. (2000). What "form" transforms? In J. Mezirow (Ed.), *Learning as transformation: Critical perspectives on a theory in progress* (pp. 35-70). San Francisco, CA: Jossey-Bass.

Kegan, R., & Lahey, L. L. (2001). The real reason people won't change. *Harvard Business Review*.

Kim, C. W., & Mauborgne, R. (2003). Fair process: Managing the knowledge economy. *Harvard Business Review*.

Lewin, K. (1947). Frontiers in group dynamics: Concept, method and reality in social science; social equilibria and social change. *Human Relations, 1*(1), 5-41. doi:10.1177/001872674700100103.

Lipmanowicz, H., & McCandless, K. (2014). *The Surprising Power of Liberating Structures: Simple rules to unleash a culture of innovation*. Seattle, WA: Liberating Structures Press.

Marrow, A. J. (1969). *The practical theorist*. New York, NY: Teachers College Press.

Marshak, R. J. (2002). Changing the language of change: How new contexts and concepts are challenging the ways we think and talk about organizational change. *Strategic Change, 11*(5), 279-282.

Marshak, R. J. (2004). Generative conversations: How to use deep listening and transforming talk in coaching and consulting. *OD Practitioner, 36*(3), 25-29.

Marshak, R. J. (2016). Anxiety and change in contemporary organization development. *Organization Development, 48*(1).

Marshak, R. J. (2020). *Dialogic process consulting: Generative meaning-making in action*. BMI Series in Dialogic OD. North Vancouver, Canada: BMI Publishing.

Merron, K. (2006). Masterful consulting. In J. V. Gallos (Ed.), *Organization Development: A Jossey-Bass Reader*. San Francisco, CA: Jossey-Bass.

Mezirow, J. (2009). Transformative learning theory. In J. Mezirow, E. W. Taylor, & and associates (Eds.), *Transformative Learning In Practice: Insights from Community, Workplace and Higher education* (pp. 18-31). San Francisco, CA: Jossey Bass.

Nexus4Change. (n.d.). Collaborative Change Library and App. Retrieved from https://nexus4change.com.

Okonkwo, J. N., & Owusu, S. J. (2016). Remembering—The gift of OD. *Organization Development Practitioner, 48*(3).

Oswick, C. (2009). Revisioning or re-versioning? A commentary on diagnostic and dialogic forms of organization development. *The Journal of Applied Behavioural Science, 45*(3), 369-374.

Presencing Institute. (2017). Theory U. from https://www.presencing.org/theoryu

Quinn, R. E. (2004). *Building the bridge as you walk on it: A guide to leading change*. San Francisco, CA: Jossey-Bass.

Ratcheva, V. S., & Leopold, T. (2018). Five things to know about the future of jobs. Retrieved from https://www.weforum.org/agenda/2018/09/future-of-jobs-2018-things-to-know/.

Riessman, C. K. (2008). *Narrative methods for the human sciences*. Thousand Oaks, CA: SAGE.

Rock, D., & Schwartz, J. (2006). The neuroscience of leadership. *Strategy+Business, Management Issues*(43), 2-10.

Rock, D. (2008). SCARF: a brain-based model for collaborating with and influencing others. NeuroLeadership Journal, (vol 1). NeuroLeadership Institute.

Roehrig, M. J., Schwendenwein, J., & Bushe, G. R. (2015). Amplifying change: A three-phase approach to model, nurture and embed ideas for change. In G. R. Bushe & R. J. Marshak (Eds.), *Dialogic Organization Development: The Theory and Practice of Transformational Change*. Oakland: CA: Berrett-Koehler.

Schein, E. (2006). Facilitative process interventions: Task process in groups. In J. V. Gallos (Ed.), *Organization Development: A Jossey-Bass Reader*. San Francisco, CA: Jossey-Bass.

Schein, E. (2013). *Humble inquiry*. San Francisco: CA: Berrett-Koehler.

Schein, E. (2015). Introduction. In G. R. Bushe & R. J. Marshak (Eds.), *Dialogic Organization Development: The Theory and Practice of Transformational Change*. Oakland: CA: Berrett-Koehler.

Schein, E. (2016). *Humble consulting*. San Franscisco: CA: Berrett-Koehler.

Schein, E. H. (1999). *Process consultation revisited: Building the helping relationship*. Reading, MA:Addison-Wesley Longman Pub.

Schwarz, R. M. (2002). *The skilled facilitator: A comprehensive resource for consultants, facilitators, managers, trainers, and coaches / Roger Schwarz* (New and rev. ed. ed.): San Francisco : Jossey-Bass.

Schwarz, R. (2006). The facilitator and other facilitative roles. In J. V. Gallos (Ed.), *Organization Development: A Jossey-Bass Reader*. San Francisco, CA: Jossey-Bass.

Seashore, C. N., Nash, M. M., Thompson, G., & Mattare, M. (2004). Doing good by knowing who you are: The instrumental self as an agent of change. *OD Practitioner, 36*(3).

Sinek, S., Mead, D., & Docker, P. (2017). *Find your why: A practical guide to discovering purpose for you and your team*. New York, NY: Penguin Random House.

Snowden, D., & Boone, M. (2007). A leader's framework for decision-making. *Harvard Business Review* (November), 69-74.

Sonenshein, S. (2010). We're changing—or are we? Untangling the role of progressive, regressive, and stability narratives during strategic change implementation. *The Academy of Management Journal, 53*(3), 477-512.

Southern, N. (2015). Framing inquiry: The art of engaging great questions. In G. R. Bushe & R. J. Marshak (Eds.), *Dialogic Organization Development: The Theory and Practice of Organizational Change*. San Francisco: CA: Berrett-Koehler.

Stralen, v. D. (2011). High reliability organizing. Retrieved from http://high-reliability.org/High-Reliability-Organizations.

Swart, C. (2013). *Re-Authoring the world: The narrative lens and practices for organizations, communities and individuals*. Sandberg, South Africa: Knowres Publishing.

Swart, C. (2015). Coaching from a dialogic OD paradigm. In G. R. Bushe & R. J. Marshak (Eds.), *Dialogic Organization Development: The Theory and Practice of Organizational Change*. San Francisco, CA: Berrett-Koehler.

Taylor, E. W., Cranton, P., & Associates (Eds.) (2012). *Handbook of transformative learning: Theory, research and practice*. San Francisco, CA: John Wiley and Sons.

van den Nieuwenhof, R. (2013). The language of change: Generativity in dialogical processes. In *Organizational Generativity: The Appreciative Inquiry Summit and a*

Scholarship of Transformation (Vol. 4, pp. 159-188): Emerald Group Publishing Limited.

Weick, K. E., & Quinn, R. E. (1999). Organization change and development. *Annual Review of Psychology, 50*, 361-386.

Wheatley, M. (2017). *Who do we choose to be?:Facing reality, claiming leadership, restoring sanity*. Oakland, CA: Berrett-Koehler.

Wheatley, M. J. (1994). *Leadership and the new science: learning about organization from an orderly universe*. San Francisco, CA : Berrett-Koehler Publishers.

Yorks, L., & Kasl, E. (2006). I know more than I can say: A taxonomy for using expressive ways of knowing to foster transformative learning. *Journal of Transformative Education, 4*(1), 43-64.

ABOUT THE AUTHOR

Dr Yabome Gilpin-Jackson considers herself a dreamer, doer and storyteller, committed to imagining and leading the futures we want. She is an applied social scientist, working in the areas of human development & leadership/organization development as a scholar, consultant, and writer. She has over 15 years' experience consulting across the private, public, and nonprofit sectors and assuming executive leadership roles in the field. Dr. Yabome Gilpin-Jackson teaches undergraduate and graduate courses in her areas of expertise. She was named an Institute for Social Innovation Scholar at Fielding Graduate University, CA for her published research into the transformational leadership of war-affected peoples from Africa and was a contributor to the ground-breaking book: *Dialogic Organization Development: The Theory and Practice of Transformational Change* (Berrett-Koehler, 2015). She has written journal articles about the Grey Zone of Change and Organization Development Practice. She has also been awarded International African Woman of the Year by UK-based Women4Africa and was the first ever recipient of the US-based Organization Development Network's Emerging Organization Development Practitioner award. In addition, she has received the prestigious Harry Jerome Professional Excellence Award in Canada.

In addition to peer-reviewed publications, she is the author of *Identities & Ancestries* short story collections about global African experiences and lead editor of the *We Will Lead Africa* series, a non-fiction anthology of everyday African leadership stories.. Yabome continues to research, write, and speak on leadership & organization development issues, posttraumatic growth, and on honouring diversity and social equality in our locally global world. Yabome is community-engaged on various Boards, including the Organization Development Network, Canadian-based NGO, The People's Foundation for Sierra Leone, and The Mayor's Advisory Board for Black History Month in Vancouver.

You can find Dr Gilpin-Jackson online at:
www.SLDConsulting.org;
Twitter: https://twitter.com/supportdevelop
Facebook: https://www.facebook.com/yabomewriter/
Amazon: https://www.amazon.com/author/yabomegilpin-jackson
Linkedin: https://www.linkedin.com/in/yabome/

Forthcoming books by Dr. Yabome Gilpin-Jackson:

- "Transformation After Trauma: The Power of Resonance," Peter Lang Publishers
- "Handbook of Learning for Transformation," Palgrave McMillan (Editorial Team Member)